GLORY (

A JOURNEY TO SELF REALIZATION

A Modern Commentary on Mandukya Upanishad

GLORY OF OM:

A JOURNEY TO SELF REALIZATION

A Modern Commentary on Mandukya Upanishad

By

Banani Ray

Inner Light Publishers
www.inner-light-in.com

Published
by

INNER LIGHT PUBLISHERS

Rishikesh, India

www.inner-light-in.com

Published 2013

ISBN: 978-9382123248

Email: innerlight.in@gmail.com

Contents

Mandukya: A Gift to the Humanity

In all ages, evolved human minds have never ceased to wander about their own Self. Who am I? Why do we exist on earth? What is the purpose of this life and what happens after death? Does God really exist? Such questions have forever haunted seekers in all cultures and religions of the world. The ancient text Mandukya Upanishad addresses such questions that hang around the mind of a seeker of Self-realization.

The wisdom of Mandukya Upanishad is the most precious knowledge ever revealed to the humankind. No other text in the history of humankind contains such a profound knowledge within such a humble scope— just twelve verses.

Mandukya Upanishad had been documented around 800—400 B.C. The book contains the most precious revelation on the nature of reality.

Mandukya Upanishad contains sacred and secret spiritual knowledge that were revealed to ancient sages who strived to know the secret of life. This ancient knowledge was carried forward and practiced by their disciples for centuries, generations after generations.

Om is the essence of the Mandukya Upanishad. Om is the sacred wisdom which the Mandukya contains and expounds. Om is the universal God. Om is our true Self, it contends. Om is that one syllable, the primordial vibration, the infinite cosmic principle, which creates, sustains and supports this Universe. Mandukya Upanishad contains all you need to know about Om, the eternal sound vibration of the existence. It contains all you need to know about your 'self', if you are seeking self-realization.

Whether you believe in personal God or not, the knowledge of Mandukya Upanishad will give you a solid base or support to rely on. It is the support of Om, the grand Universal Consciousness that supports, nourishes and nurtures this existence.

In the modern times, people have often been wary of the God preached by religions— the God created by narrow sectarian views. There had been enough bloodshed on earth in the name of God and religion than for anything else. With all their well-meaning words and intentions of love, acceptance and tolerance of others, religions have only succeeded in creating divisions between man and woman, saints and sinners, monks and householders, thereby destroying the possibility of one human race peacefully coexisting on earth with dignity and respect to the self and others.

Does a Universal God exist – the God that is neither yours, nor mine, neither Hindu, nor Muslim, nor Christian? Is there a God that exists beyond all labels, beyond the boundary of any religion or religious sect? Is there a God whom no religious group can claim as theirs? Is there a God that loves us unconditionally?

Mandukya says that that such a universal God not only exists but that God is really a living phenomena underlying you, me, our planet earth and the whole of existence. You do not need to go to any temple or church to worship God. The whole existence is God's temple. Your own body is the temple of God. Your own heart is the shrine. You do not need to subscribe to any religion to experience God. The only religion you need to experience God is love, kindness and respect to all beings. You do not need any preacher or prophet to learn about God. The teaching is spread on the trees and the mountains, on the stars and the river, on the Sun and the moon. The ultimate teaching is written in your heart. You just need to wake up and see.

Mandukya Upanishad is the most profound of all Upanishads, and it is a precious gift to humanity. Mandukya is very much life-affirming. It never condemns anyone or makes distinction between one human being and another, male or female, saint or sinner, monk or a layperson. Mandukya Upanishad upholds the highest dignity of human being. Mandukya Upanishad expounds that nobody is holier than you. You are, as everyone is, the most sacred expression of the divinity. This is an unalterable truth for saints and sinners alike, however fallen one may appear in the eyes of the world.

To the sage of the Upanishad, life is a pilgrimage. Each moment is to be lived in depth rather than superficially gliding by, because each moment contains God, hidden within it.

God is hidden within you, within me, within a bird, a flower or a butterfly. Every moment of our existence is an opportunity to discover God, the Essence, the Tao, the Presence, the Cosmic Consciousness, or the Buddha Nature— whatever you'd like to call it. This life is an opportunity to find God within us, within our fellow beings, within our surroundings. Mandukya Upanishad gives us the map, the key and the know-how.

The Mandukya Upanishad contains what is perhaps one of the most exemplary analysis of human consciousness and its relation to God, and it is one of the earliest such document that is to be found in the written records of humankind.

Mandukya does not preach a religion. It is an exposition on the existential truth of the reality we live.

The Mandukya Upanishad is not the words of the pundits, preachers, priests or the scholars. It consists of words from persons who "knew" the truth and experienced it in the first persons. It contains profound words of realization. Those were words of truth from the sages who passionately devoted their entire life in the pursuit of truth and, as a result, received the Truth as the subjective realization of the eternal laws of the Universe. That is why you will find the truth contained in it so simple, and yet so beautiful.

Mandukya Upanishad acts like the torch to the seekers who desire to know the truth, only the truth, and nothing less than the Truth. Blind faith in belief-system, ideologies, doctrine or dogma can never set us free. Only the knowledge of truth can set us free; only the knowledge of truth can liberate us from the slavery of doctrine, dogmas, blind faiths and religious sects that fail to deliver the truth.

Only the knowledge of Truth can make us fearless, blissful and free. The Mandukya Upanishad contains such truth in abundance; it contains the Truth in its entirety; it leads the seeker to the knowledge of the reality. This Truth is valid today as it was three thousand years ago when it was revealed to the sages, and it will remain valid forever. It will lead seekers from untruth to truth, from darkness to light, from death to immortality.

When you study the verses of the Mandukya and revel in its wisdom, your heart will be filled with gratitude to the person who made such wealth of wisdom available to the humankind. But it is impossible to determine who wrote the text or how many authors were engaged in its composition. The wisdom was transmitted orally for centuries to worthy seekers before being recorded in writing. So, the seer of the mantras remains unknown, but the flower of knowledge continues to spread its fragrance and it will continue to do so in the future.

We need some preparation to study the great scripture. Mandukya expounds that the glory and strength of human beings come from the truth of their oneness with the source. When you proceed to the study of Self-knowledge that this Upanishad delivers, you need a heart filled with goodwill and respect toward the creation of God, a genuine intent of peace and an open mind to enquire and receive the Truth.

In the following pages, we will discuss only the twelve original mantras of the Mandukya Upanishad to keep things simple for the modern readers. These twelve mantras of Mandukya Upanishad are enough to enlighten a human being, if pursued intelligently.

Here it should be noted that Mandukya Upanishad does contain advanced concepts which don't quite comply with our ordinary understanding. These advanced concepts are sometimes difficult to accept and assimilate with our present world-view. They can fly in the face of logic and they may even sound 'absolutist'. When we hear concepts such as: God is love, everything is God, or we are not separate beings, our mind may not seem to be ready to accept them.

However, the knowledge you are going to receive in this book is a treasure of lifetime. It is not just a metaphysical theory, but the existential truth of the universe. Sincere study of this great scripture can liberate you from all your self-imposed limitations and help you realize your real Self. Sincere study of this great Upanishad will lead the seeker to a new realm of limitless joy, fulfillment and peace, which is the zenith of human existence.

Chapter 1: The Sound that is Everything

IN THE VERY BEGINNING of creation, there was no earth, no water, no fire, no air, not even the space... There was a void—a mysterious form of vacuum — a pure nothingness containing no space, no time, no matter, no light, no sound. Yet this curious vacuum held potential for creation. It contained the seed of creation as the smallest pulsation.

You have probably known that sound or 'word' is the basis of creation. In Bible they call it 'the word'. Sages call it the Shabda Brahman— the ever-expanding field of sound. Mandukya Upanishad says Om is that sound, that creative vibration, the seed vibration. The whole existence is hidden within it, just as a giant tree is hidden within a seed. Om is the primordial sound of existence.

In reality, Om is neither a name, nor a word. The reality of Om cannot be expressed in words. The closest term it can be expressed in the language known to the humankind is Vibration. It is the primordial vibration or throb in the field of cosmic oneness that existed by itself.

Now let us begin with the Mandukya Upanishad. Let us see what the Mandukya Upanishad says about it.

The first mantra of the Mandukya Upanishad:

Verse 1: Hari Om. Om, this immortal sound, is all that exists. It is the past, it is the present and it is the future. All that exist are really expressions of Om. And whatever transcends the three spheres of time, that too is indeed Om.

This one verse says everything you need to know about Om. There are many people who chant Om, meditate on Om and loves Om. Om itself is a beautiful word, worth-loving. Om is a very much soothing and comforting word that deep-cleanses the inner debris of a human being, because, it is the eternal sound of existence-awareness-bliss. Still, few in this world know the true significance of Om. It was there in the existence, when no religion was formed or founded. It will be there in the existence, if all the religions are demolished.

Om is consciousness in its purest form. It exists as the backdrop of everything and every being in the visible and invisible Universe. Om is the signature sound of this Universe. It is the soundless sound of existence. It resounds in all that exists. It resounds in me; it resounds in you. Everything, every being is an expression of this eternal Om.

The Grand Thief

Mandukya Upanishad begins with the words "Hari Om". The word 'Hari' in Sanskrit means that which steals away. In this mantra the word 'Hari' is used as an adjective of Om. The words 'Hari Om' mean Om is the presence which steals away. Steals away what? It steals away the ordinary mundane existence of strife, struggle and duality; it steals away anxiety, aggression, fear, grief and sorrow; it steals away the debris of anger, hatred, confusion and ignorance, to fill us with the nectar of joy, immortality and life eternal. It steals away our heart, our limited self to reveal the realm of immortality.

The Great Remover of Karmic Blockages

In Hinduism, 'Hari' is a well-known and adored name of God. 'Hari' means 'the remover', — the grand Presence that removes all divisions and dualities to reveal the ground of oneness, which is divine love.

In the first verse, 'Hari' is an attribute of Om. Om is the divine love, which lovingly removes, steals all our fears and suffering. There is a deeper meaning hidden behind the use of this word. The verses of Mandukya are regarded as mantras. They are capable of cutting through the nets of illusion.

'Hari Om' means Om is 'Hari', the grand remover of sins. When one remembers Om, and repeats this mantra, all his sins, karmas and bad astrological effects steadily melt away. Pain and sufferings are also removed. Om takes away all our bad Karma and suffering; but it doesn't make a show of it. Just like a thief operates in secrecy, it secretly steals away the pains and sufferings of this world so you don't even get to know that you are being unburdened from your past.

Who else will clean us from our bad Karmas, except a God of love? Om is that God of love. Like a loving mother Om cleans us of our clutters collected through many incarnations.

This mantra of Mandukya Upanishad contains within it the cosmic vibration which removes all confusions, illusion and duality. What remains is a consciousness filled with undivided love and peace that passes all understanding. Om itself is that ground of unsurpassable beauty.

Everything is Om

The later part of the first verse says that everything contained in the domains of the past, present and future is Om. Om has expressed itself as everything, just as the water expresses itself as the bubbles, waves and foam in the ocean. The multifarious forms, textures and colors in this

Universe are all Om. Om is the things, Om is the ingredient, Om is the container and the content. There is nothing other than Om.

Anything that you are aware of is Om. You, I and all other things are essentially made of Om. Everything in the past, present and future is Om. The mind is made of Om. Thoughts are made of Om. All our emotions are made of Om. Anything that exists is made of Om. Om is the basic building block of all that exists.

Mind is Time

The first verse of the Mandukya also says that Om is time itself— past, present and the future. It is also that which exists beyond time. Time has an illusory quality about it. Sometimes we find it short and sometimes, long. In a long check-out line, or in a long traffic line up, we realize how long we find time passing. And how quickly does time fly away when we meet a long lost friend in a transit? Do you see that the perception of time is in our mind? It is our mind that interprets certain duration of time as 'long' or 'short'. When the mind is restless, time seems long. When the mind is comparatively calm, time seems short.

Mind is synonymous with time because it continuously keeps moving between the past and the future. It moves between the present location and the desired destination. This movement of mind creates the perception of time.

The Eternal Present

When the movement of mind ceases, if it happens even for a fraction of a moment, we experience that which is beyond mind, that which is timeless. Meditating on Om can bring you this seemingly impossible feat. It can give you the taste of the timeless present. This domain of timelessness will free you from the clutches of your past and the anxieties for the future.

Life is a story that we weave together from the thoughts, feelings, and emotions we experience every moment. We live the most of our life in the memories of our past and the expectations of the future. Rarely do we live in the purity of the present. Past memories and future expectations are breeding grounds of stresses and tensions that often cloud our consciousness. The mantra 'Hari Om' can help you let go of the past. 'Hari Om' can also smooth out the disturbing thoughts of the future. It helps us rest in the present with complete surrender and peace. With 'Om' as our companion and support, we remain free to make peace with the past or consciously choose our future.

BANANI RAY

Past Present and Future

Scientists as well as mystics have been using ancient concepts from the Eastern philosophy to describe the mystery of time and space.

D. T. Suzuki, Buddhist scholar and philosopher, who was instrumental in spreading Zen in the West, wrote, "In this spiritual world there are no time divisions such as past, present, future, for they have contracted themselves into a single moment of the present where life quivers in its true sense....The past and the future are rolled up in this present moment of illumination, and this present moment is not something standing still with all its contents, for it ceaselessly moves on."

In the book "The Nature of Space and Time", modern scientists Stephen Hawking and Roger Penrose attempted to solve the mystery of the flow of time by using Einstein's theory of General Relativity and modern Quantum Field Theory. They attempted to produce a new theory known as "Quantum Gravity". But the mystery behind the initial conditions at the birth of the Universe is not yet solved. Scientific deductions cannot go backward beyond the birth of the Universe, which forms the limit of our knowledge of the so called "Past".

The sage of the Upanishad says that Om is time and also that which exists beyond the domain of time. The sage of

Mandukya says that Om exists beyond the past, present and future, because it contains time within its bosom. Om is ever-fresh and ever-new.

The Timeless Elixir of Immortality

Om is the timeless, space-less reality that exists beyond our sensory perception and also beyond our mental construct of logic. The fourth and transcendental aspect of Om is the background of this Existence.

How can we contact this transcendental aspect of our being? Generally, our mind lives in the past and it projects the future. When there are no thoughts, the mind is no more. The moment you go beyond thoughts, you have gone beyond time. This domain of timelessness is the ultimate state of Om, which contains the elixir of immortality. That is the state of transcendence, called the fourth or 'Turiya', in Sanskrit. The experience of the 'Fourth' state is an experience of Om as pure silence, an emptiness which is full of blessedness.

This blessedness comes by not being identified with a body, with a thought, with an image, with a word, or anything with a form. We are essentially made of the energy of Om, and physics tells us that energy is indestructible. Om is the unchanging curtain, on which the changing panorama of the world appears and disappears as modifications of this energy.

When we feel this transcendental aspect of our existence as the subjective reality of our being, not as a result of thinking or intellectual analysis, but as a result of direct perception, we taste the nectar of immortality.

Be Still and Know

The energy aspect of Om is the energy of consciousness and consciousness is cosmic, because no physical object can cut or divide it. We are consciousness. The whole world appears on this cosmic consciousness. Consciousness is also Love, because it holds all that exist in perfect oneness. This Cosmic consciousness is God. Cosmic consciousness also exists within you, me and every being. Only we have forgotten to access it. How to access it? Be still and know that you are God.

Chapter 2: Om: The Signature of the Infinite

In the preceding chapter, we have learnt that Om is the basic ingredient of this cosmos, microcosm as well as macrocosm. From the next verse, the sage of the Mandukya Upanishad explores about the nature of the Self.

Who Am I?

Who or what am I? Who or what are we? This is the eternal question of a spiritual heart. The word Self literally means who we really are. Don't we know who we are? In the discussion that is about to follow, we'll see that most of us really do not know who we truly are. We are indeed ignorant of our real Self. This ignorance of our true nature is really a form of forgetfulness. In the heart of our hearts, we all know who we are. But somehow this knowledge has been forgotten, buried in oblivion. Mandukya will help us to awaken to our real Self-nature of peace and bliss.

Ordinarily, we think that we are our body. Or, at the best, we think we are the thinker of our thoughts. We experience the fatness or slimness of the body and say, "I am fat", or "I am slim"; we experience our body and mind working to heal the sick, and we say, "I am a doctor". We find our body and mind working in a profession that needs sharing our knowledge with others, and we say, "I am a teacher";

we experience abundance or lack of certain things in our environment and say, "I am rich", or "Poor", and so it goes on.

Are we really these limited beings that we feel ourselves in our everyday lives? The evolution of human consciousness has always been deeply concerned with the aspiration of breaking the constraints of the limited conditions. The main obstacle to achieve the integration with the limitless consciousness is the powerful daily identification with ego structures, personal history, and past conditioning. Interaction with the world around us reinforces this powerful identification with our seemingly limited self. Are we limited by our body, thoughts, emotions or actions? Let us see what the Mandukya has to say on this.

The second verse of Mandukya Upanishad says:

Verse 2: All this is verily Brahman, the Infinite Whole. This Self is Brahman, the infinite Whole. This Self has four states.

The second verse of Mandukya Upanishad teaches that everything in this phenomenal world is Brahman, the Infinite cosmic consciousness. In the first verse we learnt that everything is Om. So, we can infer that Om is another name of Brahman, the infinite cosmic whole. In Sanskrit they call it *'Shabda Brahman,'* which translates as the sound that is infinite.

Brahman: The Infinite and Alive Cosmic Whole

The Sanskrit word Brahman is made up of two words: BRIH (which means Great, all-pervading or Infinite) + MANAS (which means the mind or consciousness); so the word Brahman literally means 'infinite mind' or 'Cosmic Consciousness'. So, here the sage of Mandukya is speaking of a Cosmos that is alive and conscious.

When the sage of the Upanishad says, everything is Brahman, what does it mean? It means that Brahman, the infinite consciousness, is both immanent and transcendent. It is indwelling and all-pervading and it is also unaffected by the apparent modifications of forms.

This Self is Brahman: Thou Art That

The second verse of the Mandukya also says that the self, which we subjectively experience as "I am", is Brahman. It is the infinite cosmic consciousness. It means that Brahman, the infinite mind, the life-eternal, is expressing itself as this temporal existence, as you and me!

You are Brahman, as am I. We are the infinite Om. How is it possible? Our rational mind will object. How tiny we are compared to the infinite universe!

Think about a wave, which is an inseparable part of the ocean and hence, can be called the ocean itself. We can point to a wave and call it the ocean, because it is inseparably connected to the ocean in length and depth. Just so, we as individual beings are infinite too. We are inseparable part of this infinite existence. We are veritable manifestations of the great cosmic being. This is what the second verse of the Mandukya says.

Now does that seem logical? Theoretically, yes. Because everything in this existence is Brahman, the infinite Whole, it is an easy conclusion that the Self too must be Brahman, the infinite Whole. But when we think of our small self-centered everyday existence, this sentence seems too far from true.

How can we believe ourselves as Brahman, the infinite cosmic consciousness? Our mind laughs, objects and even shrink at the thought. If we are the infinite whole, then why don't we feel so? Why do we perceive ourselves as limited beings trapped within the body spanning from head to feet? Or even worse, humans often feel themselves *as* the body. Why does our ordinary perception go against the wisdom of the sages? What went wrong with us?

Our Senses Deceive Us

The answer is that our senses deceive us to perceive ourselves and others as finite beings trapped within the boundary of the skin, from head to feet.

The reality is: we are infinite. We are infinite as the energy of consciousness. Our sense organs block the reality from us. Our sensory perceptions do not give us the correct picture. Limited as they are, everything they project is limitation. Our eyes can only see things that are greater than certain measure. Our ears can only hear sounds that fall in the range of 20 Hz. To 20,000 Hz. Anything beyond this range, and our senses are incapable to report those things. How can a limited instrument capture what is limitless and infinite? Our senses can never provide us the correct vision— the vision of our infinite and all pervading being.

However, there is a reason why we perceive ourselves as we do. If we could always perceive our infinite nature, it would be almost impossible for us to become engaged with the world. Therefore our sense organs are designed in such a way that we perceive ourselves as limited beings.

Wake Up and See

However, the fact remains that ordinarily we create our misery by thinking ourselves as limited beings. We live our life obsessed with the notion of our individuality, and we keep generating various emotions such as anger, hatred or fear, when we feel 'another limited being' is intruding upon or interfering with our freedom of peaceful existence. This chronic notion of division between the self and the other makes us miserable.

This happens because our real Self is invisible and imperceptible to our senses. We are unable to perceive us as the indivisible ground of pure consciousness, though it is the most intimate and innate truth of our being. We are unable to perceive us as pure consciousness because our mind is full of thoughts most of the time and it seldom becomes silent to allow us a glimpse of the truth.

Now, in the second verse, the sage of Mandukya exhorts us to realize our infinite nature. This verse of Mandukya Upanishad has the potential to wake us up from the hypnotic idea that we are limited beings.

Repeated reading and contemplating on this verse of Mandukya Upanishad can make the intellect pure and thus remind us that we are the pure and limitless Self. We can never be anything other than the unchanging consciousness that shines here and now. Nothing can diminish us. Nothing, no event, can take it away from us because here and now we are this fullness that can be experienced as being, awareness and bliss.

When we go beyond the personal story of our lives, our limited selves drop away and we experience oneness with all lives on earth; we feel our true self as cosmic. Mandukya is leading us to a hallowed ground of oneness, wherein everything and every being are inseparably connected with one another.

The Causes of Suffering

The verses of the Mandukya carry a very straightforward and simple logic. Everything is Om, the cosmic consciousness and the individual self is also the same consciousness. What does it mean? It means that we are infinite. This is the truth. But this simple statement confounds our intellect with a barrage of questions. If we are the sacred Om, and we are infinite in nature, why do we experience pain, misery or disharmonies in life? Why strife, disease and despair exist in the world?

The sages have answers to such questions. They say that old age and death are inevitable aspects of the limited existence. Whatever has a beginning must also have an end. And if you speak of the miseries born from strife and disharmony, those things exist because we have been too much focused on the false perception of limitedness that our sense organs present us with. Strife exists just because we have lost our vision of oneness. Disharmony exists because of our forgetfulness of our interconnected and infinite essence. We have lost the consciousness of our wholeness, while the reality is that there is nothing in this physical or material world that can divide the unified field of our one and infinite consciousness. It is only our mental notions that form boundaries and blockages by the fictitious idea of separation, which becomes the breeding ground of negativity, tension and suffering.

Blockages in the Energy Body

Health and harmony comes from the consciousness of oneness, which is another name of Wholeness. Diseases and disharmony are temporary disturbances in the unified field of the universal energy of Om. They appear as blockages in our energy bodies. Such blockages appear because we store life experiences, thoughts and emotions as specific energy patterns in our energy bodies. Some of those experiences, especially negative ones like anger, hatred and the like create blockages, interrupting the free flow of energy in our bodies and in our lives.

The other factor that inhibits the free flow of energy in the system is the fact that that most people live their lives at the "survival" mode of operation, which exhibits as the mental states of resistance, aggression, offense, judgment, fear and insecurity. Such states arise out of the limited thinking that springs from the thoughts of our limited being. This too creates blockages and the excess energy in the system become stale, giving rise to many diseases in the body and disharmony in the life.

Return to Love

Wholeness is the remedy to all ills we have created in our lives and in the world. Om is the God; Om is Love; Om is the Ground of Oneness. We may call it by whatever name we like. But we need to return to Om to heal ourselves and our lives. The disturbances in the energy-field can be smoothed out by living our life at the level of Om, by living at the ground of oneness and by attuning to Om, the eternal music of our being. Om is that eternal music which can smooth away all the creases of negativity in our Karmic database. It is that divine elixir that can clear away all the obstructions in our energy bodies.

All the discomforts, diseases or maladies of our life are born out of the idea of limitedness or restrictedness. Om, being the signature of the Infinite and whole, throws out this restriction or limitation.

Virtually, all Healing is about becoming whole. Om is the cosmic sound of wholeness. Thus, Om can be a great healing force in our lives. Chanting or listening to Om directly acts on our energy bodies. It can cure and heal all diseases and maladies, when done correctly. Om can serve as a vibrational bridge to holistically re-integrate the physical, mental, emotional and spiritual aspects of our being. Mental chanting of Om can release blockages in our energy bodies, and thus assist us to connect with the

Source. Meditation on Om also helps to expand our consciousness.

Om chanting and meditation can help us to raise our energy level from the basic survival mode to the level of optimum dynamism of spirit, so that we have the energy at our disposal to heal ourselves and be a great healing force in the world.

In order to allow the power of Om to take over us, we need to abandon all conditioned notions and dogmatic ideas. Only when we are open, ready and receptive in our hearts, we are able to attune with Om. Only then we are blessed with peace, health, harmonious social relationships, and oneness with the Divine Spirit.

This second mantra of Mandukya Upanishad gives us the recipe of healing all the disturbances of life. By allowing Om to take over us, we go back to the truth of our wholeness. We are healed.

When you meditate on the great and infinite Spirit, you find peace, calm and inner joy that life can bring you. When we realize the indivisible unity of life, we see nothing else, hear nothing else, and know nothing else— nothing that can create disturbance in our field of consciousness. All seemingly separate fragments fall in the indivisible web of interconnectedness. That is the blessed state of the Infinite.

Quantum Physics and Mandukya Upanishad

However, we are socially conditioned from our birth to think ourselves as bodies. Hence, when we are confronted with the truth which tells us that we are not this limited body, we are often faced with resistance in our mind for understandable reason. How to accept that you are not this limited body, when all your senses tell you so eloquently that you are this body or at the most, this body is the boundary within which you exist?

In the earlier ages there was no other way except to meditate and quiet your mind to experience the truth as your own subjective understanding. Seekers of Self-knowledge pursued this truth with diligent study, debate and reasoning, apart from meditation in seclusion. Only when you know yourself as neither this body nor the mind, you could conceive yourself as infinite consciousness.

Nowadays the progress in the field of physical sciences has made the idea at least intelligible. And once you are intellectually convinced, the work becomes less arduous. A little knowledge of the Quantum Physics will tell you that everything in this Universe is energy, and matter is not as solid as we perceive it to be.

Things appear different in forms and textures because of the difference in the frequency they vibrate on. We can take the example of ice, water and steam, (which are different expressions of the same water, or H_2O) to clarify the concept.

From this, you can infer that at the deepest level of our existence, we are not separate as a body or as a soul, because, basically, we are energy-beings connected to each other by this inseparable field of energy. Matter is energy, as spirit is.

In a Universe, where everything exists as energy, ultimately there is no line of demarcation. We exist as a unifying ground of energy. We exist as a whole, and we are infinite. Now, in the light of this scientific understanding, do the verses of Mandukya Upanishad make sense? Surely they do.

Our own subjective experience tells us that we are conscious beings. So, the energy that manifests as our earthly being must be essentially the energy of consciousness.

The quantum physicists also speak about this field of consciousness. In Quantum physics, consciousness is seen as a unified field where everything is everything else. Theory of Everything dissolves the notion of boundaries that separate one thing from another. It opens up a fascinating reality to us, where there is no 'this' or 'that,' and no 'you' or 'me'. Everything exists as indivisible part of a pure field of awareness. Everything is made of the unified field of consciousness.

Many names have been given to this unified field: the Matrix (Planck), Nature's Mind (Dr Edgar Mitchell), The Mind of God (Steven Hawking), The Field (Lynn McTaggert) and The Divine Matrix (Gregg Braden). This unified field is the intelligent field of energy that pervades everything in the Universe.

The qualities of the unified field as described by some physicists are as follows: source of all possibility, infinite organizing power, Self-awareness, infinite correlation, infinite creativity, perfect balance and self-sufficiency. In Vedic literature, such qualities are attributed to Brahman. In the Vedic literature, this unified field is referred to as the infinite cosmic consciousness.

The Living God

With the knowledge of quantum physics, a new paradigm emerges up that can heal and smooth out all ideas of separation, divisions and barricades. The dilemma whether you are a 'body' or 'not a body' can be solved just by changing your perception, by seeing your body as a mass of energy. It is easy to recognize your body, mind and deeper level of being as pure energy that vibrates at different frequencies at different levels. Even the space that you look at is teeming with the energy of consciousness.

With this knowledge, human consciousness is going through a radical change. Since any idea of separation also contradicts with the findings of the Quantum physics, which says that the Unified field contains everything within it, and nothing exists outside of it, the idea of God as a separate being no longer seems logical. The old idea that there is a creator God apart from us is becoming obsolete with the advent of this new knowledge. The old idea of God as a separate individual being is giving way to the more rational idea of God as a field of consciousness existing within us.

The God that exists as your most intimate core of being sounds to be more appropriate and emotionally acceptable, because only such a God will completely understand us and accept us as we are. The verses of Mandukya support this new paradigm.

Mandukya points us to a living and loving God, a divine presence, that exists within you and me. The God that exists within you and me as our very Self can love and accept us in spite of all our faults and weaknesses. Only such a God can understand all our limitations, compulsions and frailties, and hence love us in spite of our apparent faults or weaknesses. Only to the God, who exists within us, we can feel completely loved, assured and accepted. There can be no better God than this, and Mandukya says that such is the nature of reality. Om is God, and God exists within us as our real Self, our highest Self.

Om and the Four States of Consciousness

This verse says that Om, our real Self manifests as four states of consciousness. Self has four states, because we can experience ourselves at these four levels. Ordinarily, most of us are familiar with three states: the waking state, the dream state and the state of deep sleep. The fourth state is unknown to most of us. It is only known to the sages, yogis and those who have experienced very deep states of meditation.

For now we'll limit our discussion to only three ordinary states of consciousness that we experience every day of our life. Though we think we know these three states, do we really know them? Normally we just assume that the waking state exists independent of the other two states. We think that the waking-state- self is our real self, the dream state is unreal, and ordinarily we have no knowledge about the deep sleep state.

Do you know that the self of your dream state seems just as real so long as your dream continues? If you remember your dreams when you wake up, you will know that no dream, however absurd it might be, does seem absurd during the dream state. On the contrary it all seems very real— so real that you may feel the trepidation in your heart even when you wake up, being chased by a tiger in your dream.

Did you ever ponder why any two of these three states of our consciousness never appear together? In fact one comes when another is over. What does that mean? It means none of these states exist independent of the others, as we normally assume. It means one state gets converted into another and they keep rotating. It also means that you need to take in to account of all these states together to get a clear understanding of your real self.

Which State is Our True Self?

Mandukya Upanishad contains the most spectacular analysis of the states of our consciousness. In the next verses, we'll delve more deeply in to the three ordinary states of consciousness.

Normally we think ourselves as the limited self that we experience during our waking state. Obviously, this is a very partial knowledge of the reality, if we take in to account of all three states through which we move daily. What if someone tells you that the waking state too is a dream that is recurring back again and again?

There is a famous anecdote of a Zen monk, who dreamt that he was a butterfly. He was very happy living the life of the butterfly, deeply involved in its details when he suddenly woke up from his dream. The memory of his dream was so vivid in his mind—all those pleasures and pains of the butterfly-life, that he was in a dazed state for a long while. He began asking his disciples: Which is true? Am I a man who was dreaming that I was a butterfly? Or am I a butterfly now dreaming that I am a man?

Humorous though it sounds, knowing our dreams vividly will help us to wake up to another sort of reality that we live daily when we are asleep. To know ourselves fully, we need to know all the states of our consciousness. Then we realize who we really are.

Then we understand that we are consciousness going through all these modifications called the waking, dream and deep sleep. All states of our consciousness, the waking, dream and deep sleep are interlinked and connected with each other.

Chapter 3: Om: The Eternal Now

Following the footsteps of the sage of Mandukya Upanishad we discover a new face of reality, which to our surprise had always been there, just waiting to be seen. Everywhere there is the face of Divinity. Everything is Om and everything is Brahman, the all-pervading, Infinite, here and now. When we look out at the world with this awareness, no longer we see the world as we had known it before.

Wherever we look we see only the one Brahman, the infinite, which is the all-pervading, one consciousness. There is nothing else. Every being is already free, as everything is Brahman, the infinite consciousness.

The Waking Reality

Mandukya says that the Self expresses itself as four states, of which the waking state is the foremost. It means Om is the eternal now, which shines as every moment of our waking state. What does this moment consist of? It consists of what we are experiencing here and now. What falls in the domain of here and now? The experience of here and now begins with our body. The energy of Om is flowing in our body, in our thoughts, emotions and feelings.

This moment is an expression of the energy of Om. The third verse of Mandukya Upanishad explores the Self in the waking state.

Verse 3: The field of waking state is conscious about the externals. It has seven limbs and nineteen receptors. It receives, consumes and enjoys gross subjects (sensory inputs). This first state is known as Vaishvanara.

This verse makes us explore our waking state in great details, because normally people think that they are the body-thoughts-emotions complex that they experiences during their waking state. Actually the waking state too is a field of experience, just like our dream state. All we experience in the waking state is an expression of the Self, which is the indivisible ground of consciousness, the Brahman, according to the verse 2 of Mandukya.

How Do We Enjoy the World?

The third verse of the Mandukya Upanishad says that the Self in the waking state enjoys objects that are gross in nature. In the waking state, our consciousness is turned outward and the conscious mind is in operation. And how does the self enjoy the objects in the waking state? Through seven limbs and nineteen mouths or gates, the verse enlightens.

The Seven Limbs or Parts

The Sanskrit word *'Anga'* means limbs or parts. There are seven invisible parts or limbs, which help the body to operate, and also enjoy the world. And there are seven visible limbs that help the body to operate, and enjoy the world. The seven 'limbs' literally refers to the seven visible limbs of the body, namely, the head, neck, torso, hands, legs, anus and the genital. These parts include five organs of action (*Karmendriya*) and also the five sense organs (*Jnanendriya*).

The body can also be divided in to seven invisible parts. Seven energy centers situated in the subtle body along the torso, head and neck are the seven invisible limbs or parts, through which the Self, experience the whole gamut of experiences possible in the human body. These seven centers are situated along the spine in the head, neck and the torso. They are as follows.

1) Along the spine, in the coccyx region there is the area called Muladhara in Sanskrit, which means 'the main support'. This center is also called the root chakra, as this center supports the immunity and integrity of our whole psychosomatic system. The maintenance of our skeletal,

marrow and lymphatic system depends on this center. It is the plane that stores memory and Karmic experiences, which flowers at specific situation or stimulus. This center also controls the feeling of wellbeing. Physically, this center governs the action of elimination or excretion.

2) Up along the spine, in the area between the coccyx and navel, and along the waistline, is situated the second center, called Swadhisthana in Sanskrit, which means 'own abode'. This is the center of calmness and peace. This place is the seat of mind, according to ancient yoga text. If this center is disturbed, insecurity, anxiety and depression result. Physically, this center governs the action of procreation.

3) Up along the spine, at the level of navel is the area called Manipura in Sanskrit, meaning 'the city of jewel'. This part in human is the seat of life energy or vital force. Also known as the solar plexus, this center governs assimilation of knowledge and information and generates creative ideas for the authors and poets. If this part becomes weak or imbalanced, fear and stress results. Physically this center governs digestion. This center also governs the sense of balance and equilibrium.

4) Up along the spine, the area behind the heart is called Anahata in Sanskrit, which means 'that which is never hurt'. This part in human is the center of the witnessing silence. From this center 'Om' as the un-struck sound is

continuously emanating. Only the Yogis and mystics are able to hear this sound through subtle sense. If this center becomes weak, diseases of heart results and the breathing pattern becomes disturbed. Anger and hatred, grasping or resistances disturb this center. Physically this center governs the respiratory function and the flow of blood in the body.

5) Up along the spine, the area at the level of the base of throat is called Vishuddhi in Sanskrit, which means 'purification'. This place purifies the raw emotional energy, before it goes up. Imbalance in this center causes thyroid problem and hoarseness of voice or loss of speech. Physically this part in humans governs the speech.

6) Up along the spine, where the spine ends, behind the center of the eyebrows in the medulla oblongata region of the brain, is located the center called Ajna, in Sanskrit which means 'the place of command'. This region is the place of pituitary gland, the master gland which via controlling the other endocrine glands virtually controls the whole body and mind. This center governs the intellect, which directs our thoughts and emotions. This center is responsible for wisdom and leadership. Disturbance in this center can make people overly reactive, controlling, egoistic or dominating.

7) The seventh center is located at the top of the forehead, and is known as the crown chakra, or Sahasrar in Sanskrit. The word 'Sahasrar' also means 'the lotus of thousand petals'. This center is the place for cosmic consciousness and transcendence. Normally, for most people, this chakra remains closed for their lifetime. When this chakra opens up through spiritual practices, the consciousness flows in thousand streams and becomes one with the cosmic ocean of unified awareness. Opening of the petals of the Sahasrar brings the experience of pure silence and ultimate blessedness, bliss and peace. This center remains fully open and operative in new-born babies, but it gets almost closed when we grow up and learn to confine ourselves in hard shells of individuality.

These are the seven centers, seven important parts in human body. All our experiences or enjoyments happen through one or another of these subtle energy centers in the body.

The third verse of the Mandukya Upanishad says that apart from these seven limbs, there are nineteen gates or 'mouths', which use to bring us the experience of this world in the waking state.

What are these 19 gates? Following are the nineteen mouths, which the Self uses to receive impressions from the external world.

Gate (1-8): The first eight 'mouths' or gates are the following: The five sense organs (two eyes, two ears, two nostrils, tongue and the pores of the skin).These gates are used as entrance or portals of reception. They are used to receive the guests, viz., impressions and experiences of the external world. Experiences through these gates are as follows: seeing, hearing, smelling, breathing, tasting and touching. Sceneries, visual objects or visions, sounds, talks or music, fragrances or odors, foods or drinks and touch are the things enjoyed by these gates.

Gate (9-14): The next six gates or 'mouths' are: The palms of two hands, two soles of the feet (subtle openings exist in those apparently solid places), the anus, and the genital. Through these gates, the Self experiences the elements of this universe like earth, water, air, fire and space and also interacts with the environment.

Gate (15-18): The next four gates belong to the mind. These are situated in the subtle or mental body. They are as follows:

i) Thinking faculty, called Manas in Sanskrit; it creates thoughts, and sends and receives thought signals from the environment. It is physically situated below the navel, in the lower abdomen.

ii) Discriminating faculty, called Buddhi in Sanskrit. It discriminates between good and bad and helps us to make choices between things, persons or situations. Physically this faculty is situated in the heart area. Through this mouth the Self also experiences love or hatred, pleasure and pain.

iii) Storing faculty, called Chitta, in Sanskrit. It stores thoughts and impressions and emits or brings up the past thoughts and impressions when they are exposed to or stimulated by favorable environment. This center is physically situated in the area around the coccyx. Through this mouth the Self enjoys and experiences memories—good or bad.

iv) Ego or the possessing faculty, called Ahamkara, or maker of the 'I'. This faculty takes the possession of thoughts, impressions, deeds, and experiences them as "me" or "mine". It assumes doer-ship of all thoughts and actions and enjoys and suffers accordingly. Physically, this center is situated in the area between the eyebrows.

Gate 19: This mouth is situated at the top of the head. It is our cosmic connection that keeps us alive. Through this gate or mouth, we enjoy silence, meditation, Samadhi and all the things or experiences that seem 'otherworldly' or 'divine'.

So, these are the nineteen gates, which enable the Self to enjoy and experience the world, in the waking state. This information is not just intellectual information; they are necessary, if you really want to understand yourself.

Knowledge is power. When you know how your body and mind work, you get to know your true reality and you get power over them. Knowing yourself is empowering. You get power over your destiny, when you know who or what you really are. The Mandukya Upanishad provides you the key.

How does this knowledge help us? This knowledge helps you to dis-identify with your body. When you deeply study yourself (which is called Swadhyaya— means self study), you know that your body-mind complex is just like a vehicle, or a sophisticated bio-computer that is used to store, produce, retrieve, receive and send data (thoughts, emotions and experiences) on contact with the external world. In ancient texts like the Bhagvad Gita, this body is called a city. Just like a city, it has gates or ports (points of entrances and exits), which are used to send and receive information to and fro.

There is another advantage of studying our waking, dream and deep sleep states. When you know that the field of your waking state is a just a partial expression of your own Self, your identification with your small self lessens. You know that your body is just a small fragment of the field of your waking-state consciousness— the field, which consists of the whole existence. We are consciousness, the whole. We are not even only the waking consciousness; we are the whole, which also include the dream state consciousness, the deep sleep and the background of all experiences. We are the energy of Om.

Vaishvanara: The Cosmic Human

This verse of Mandukya says that the waking state of the Self is also known as the *Vaishvanara*, which means the cosmic human. When you understand that your body is made up of your own consciousness, everything else you are conscious of is also made of your own consciousness. This helps you to infer that the whole Universe that you experience in your waking state is made of your waking state consciousness, which include your body among the other things and beings.

This understanding can be developed by a practice called the *Vaishvanara* meditation. In this meditation, you begin by knowing the cosmos as your own body. You are the cosmic space of consciousness that supports the whole Universe, of which your body is just a tiny part. There is nothing in the cosmos which does not form an organic part of your cosmic body. Your real Self in the waking state is *Vaishvanara*, the cosmic being. This is the message of this verse of Mandukya Upanishad. The individual body and mind is actually an infinitesimal part of this *Vaishvanara*— the cosmic being.

Chapter 4: Mystery of Dream and Deep Sleep

Entire teachings of the Mandukya Upanishad is saturated with and permeated by the knowledge of Om. If you know Om in theory and practice, you will know the ground-consciousness that supports our existence; then you will come to know all the mysteries of life and death. You'll come to know the loving and living God that supports, nurtures and nourishes our individual bodies and minds.

When you will know all the mysteries of the waking, dream and deep sleep, you will know the mysteries of the Universe. You will see that your life is truly a seamless web of transitory states of consciousness, where the waking state effortlessly merges with the dream state, and the dream state effortlessly merges into deep sleep. From the state of deep sleep again you emerge to be the self in the dream state and then enter the waking state.

In deep sleep, there is no form, no feelings, no words, no desires, and no movie. There is only the luminous screen, covered by a curtain of unawareness, which covers its effulgence. As we come back from the deep sleep to the dream state, immediately we find ourselves in the midst of a story involving a world of people and objects. It is also the same with the waking state.

However the whole process of transition from waking to dream to deep sleep, and again from deep sleep to dream to the waking is very smooth. There is no jerk in the process. The whole process is so smooth and perfect that we seldom wonder about it. We seldom wonder why we dream what we dream and why dreams use to be there. We seldom wonder why the dreams seem so 'realistic', while we are dreaming. We seldom wonder why we do not question the reality of a dream when we are dreaming, even if they seem absurd when we wake up.

As a means of exploring the Self, the Mandukya Upanishad makes us conscious of the three ordinary states of our consciousness, and also tells us that there is a fourth state. The fourth verse of the Mandukya Upanishad talks about the dream state, which, it says, is another expression of the Self.

The fourth verse of Mandukya Upanishad says:

Verse 4: In the Dream state, the Self is conscious about the   inner world. This second state is known as the Taijasa. It operates through seven limbs and nineteen gates to experience and enjoy the subtle objects of the mental realm.

Mandukya says that our dream state too is an expression of the Self, like the waking state. Dream state is also made of the energy of consciousness, and the energy of consciousness is the energy of Om. The Upanishad says that in the dream state too, the Self operates through the seven 'limbs' and enjoys (or suffer, if it is a nightmare) experiences through the nineteen gates of the subtle body, which we discussed in the preceding chapter.

The Dream World

While we are in the waking state of consciousness, the consciousness operates through the conscious mind, which collects information through the sense organs and interprets the collected sensory input on the basis of the feelings of pleasure, pain or neutrality of the experiences. While we are asleep, the conscious mind shuts down and the external sense organs no longer operate. In the dream state, our consciousness operates at the level of the unconscious mind, which is a storehouse of past impressions.

In dream state, our consciousness actually turns inward and it experiences the objects of mind that are stored as subtle impressions at the level of unconscious mind. For every sense organ in our physical body, there is a subtle counterpart existing in the subtle body, which is the unconscious mind.

When the conscious mind shuts down, the unconscious mind begins to operate and the subtle counterparts of the sense organs come in to operation. This is the reason why we experience the dream world almost the same way as we do in our waking state. We smell, taste, touch, hear and see things and interact with our environment in our dreams. You know it, if you are able to remember your dream when you wake up.

Often people do not remember their dreams when they wake up. This is why you'll often hear people saying: 'I do not have dreams'. This is almost impossible. Only a Buddha can remain aware in his or her sleep. Their sleep has a different quality altogether, unknown to ordinary consciousness.

Scientists discovered that normally, most people over the age of 10 dreams at least 4 to 6 times per night during a stage of sleep called REM (Rapid Eye Movements, a distinguishing characteristic of dream stage of sleep). They also discovered that majority of our dreams relate to our everyday settings, characters, and activities.

Why Do We Dream?

Each night, we spend about one and a half to two hours dreaming. We dream about once every 90 minutes of sleep. The time you spend in dreams throughout the night, varies from about 10 minutes to around 45 minutes or slightly longer. But no one is sure why we dream. Many psychologists are of the opinion that dreams are reflections of unfulfilled desires, hopes, expectations or deep seated fears. Your dream world actually conveys the picture of your unconscious mind, which is a part of the collective unconscious mind.

Modern scientists have defined a dream as a form of thinking that occurs when (a) there is a certain minimal level of brain activation, and (b) external stimuli are blocked from entry into the mind.

Going in to the analysis of the dream state, the Māndūkya Upanishad says that the Self enjoys the subtle objects and experiences of the inner world with the help of seven limbs and nineteen 'mouths' just the same as it does during the waking state. In dream state, the consciousness enjoys the dream objects through dream limbs or organs.

Aware Dreaming

Dreams can be a great source of insight in your life. When you know your dreams, you know the content of your unconscious mind. During your dreams, if you know that you are dreaming, even the worst dream experiences cannot frighten you as much, and you can enjoy the good dream experiences like you enjoy a movie. In modern times this practice is often termed as 'lucid dreaming'. Many of you might have often experienced this. During a dream, you suspect that you are dreaming and you just wake up.

If you remember your dream when you wake up and make a note of it, within a few days, you will see that there is not much difference between the waking and dream state consciousness, except for the fact that the waking state recurs repeatedly and is perceived to last for a relatively long duration. In fact, during the dream, the time and space within a dream experience seems to be as real as they appear in the waking state.

Similarity between the Two States

Normally, we regard dreams as unreal and waking state as real. However, if you examine your dreams a little, you will be amazed to find that during your dream, you have a dream body, which you think 'real', so long as the dream lasts. Just as in your waking state you have a body, with which you completely identify with the thoughts such as "This is me", during your dream too, you have a dream body with which you completely identify through thoughts such as "This is me". The identification lasts so long as the dream lasts.

If you remember your dreams, you'll know that the forms and phenomena of the dream are perceived as much defined, solid and real as the forms and phenomena in the waking state are. During your dream state, your waking body disappears from your consciousness, just as during the waking state the dream body disappears. Do you see that there are similarities between your waking and dream state?

Waking Vs. Dream Reality

Our dreams can be source of enlightenment, if we try to remember our dream and practice awareness to such an extent that we remain aware even during the dream. There is a form of spiritual practice, which encourages you to try to remain conscious while you are dreaming. There is a stage in this practice where your inner being begins to awake. This results in a sort of witness attitude that makes you look at all experiences as a spectator or observer, observing things happening within your body and mind, and outside of your body and mind but taking no active interest in them.

However, dreams are just dreams and waking state seems so real in comparison that it can be difficult to be convinced that two states are similar. The main reason why the waking state seems more real than a dream is that the waking state recurs repeatedly throughout our lives and they are so consistent compared to dreams.

There is no doubt that the waking objects appear to be of more practical value than the dream objects by a comparison of the two states. The waking state self seems more solid and real because every day we wake up to find almost the same self and the same reality; there is apparently no discontinuity. But still there is scope for doubt. If you ask yourself who is making this comparison between the waking and dream state, you will find that the answer is: Our waking self.

Now, a scientific observation requires that the observer should stand alone apart from the objects of observation. Only then the comparison can gain neutrality and become free from personal bias. Here in our analysis, what are the objects of observation? 1) The self in the waking state and 2) the self in the dream state. And who is the observer? The self in the waking state is the observer. The object of observation itself has become the observer!

This is the famous conundrum, acknowledged by the Quantum physicists. In a world where observer is part of the observed phenomena, how can the observation give us unbiased and truthful conclusion? So, we have to acknowledge that when we conclude and assert that the waking state self is our real self and dreams are unreal, there is a possibility of a vain and biased conclusion.

Just as a judge in a court does not belong to either party contending, the one that makes a comparison between the waking and dreaming states cannot belong to either of the states. No comparison of any kind is possible, unless one has learnt to withdraw from both of these states and objectively observed them as a witness, as the sage of the Mandukya did.

Which One is Real?

There is a story of the enlightened king Janaka. Just before his enlightenment, one night he went through a funny loop of dream series. Each one of his dreams was more vivid than the previous one. In each dream his dream personality started dreaming another dream. Dream within a dream!

His dreams were scary and he had a series of waking ups, only to find him as another dream personality. Ultimately when he woke up to his current reality as the king Janaka, he began to doubt if that too was another dream! He began to doubt his current reality, which so far he had known as 'real'.

His doubt didn't leave him after several days and months, because, in his dreams he spent long spans of months and years, only to wake up after an instant and find his vivid dream experience of 'years' to be a false perception of time. His dream experience had shaken him so thoroughly that he started asking everybody this apparently funny question: "Which one is real? This one, or that one?" The scholars of his court had no clue about how to pacify their king. His ministers were sorry to see the sad plight of their king.

Everywhere on the land rumors spread about the troubled mental state of the king. Ultimately, the rumor reached the wisest person of the land. He was a sage named Ashtavakra. Ashtavakra decided to visit the king in his court. When he came to Janaka, the king courteously offered him a seat and asked the same question he had been asking everyone for the past few days.

"Which one is real? This one or that one?"

Astavakra smiled and said, "Nothing is real, o King! Neither this one, nor that one!" A flame of inner understanding transpired between the sage and the king, and Janaka finally found the answer to his question. He became a disciple to sage Ashtavakra, to study the science of self-realization.

The True Face of Reality

Have you ever wondered where did all the people and objects of your dream exist? What were they made of?

Where did they vanish when the dream ended? All those things seemed to be so solid and real during your dream! They existed nowhere but in the space of your own consciousness. They were made up of nothing but the substance or emptiness of your own consciousness. They vanished nowhere but in to your own consciousness.

Just so, is it possible that this waking state too is a dream, a long dream? Is it possible that this body and all other bodies and things that you experience as 'real' are not as real as you think? Is it possible that they are really dream bodies and dream objects that are made of the substance or non-substance emptiness of your own consciousness? Is it possible that they are happening in the space of your own consciousness, which has no shape, form or color of its own?

The sages say that it is not only possible; it is the Truth. It is the true nature of the reality, if you care to know what the truth or reality is! The enlightened ones of all ages endorse this from their subjective experience and realization, be it an Ashtavakra, a Buddha or the sage of the Mandukya Upanishad.

Deep Sleep: Return to Our Peaceful Source

Now let us explore the state of deep sleep. Of the three states (waking, dream and deep sleep), it is the most peaceful state of existence. For common people who normally live in an identified state of consciousness, deep sleep is the state where the Self is closest to its real nature of pure silence. In deep sleep, the small self ceases to assert itself, and there is no form or phenomena to identify with. Hence this state rejuvenates and refreshes the body and mind so much. In deep sleep, our consciousness becomes free of forms and it becomes one with its formless essence, which is called the pure consciousness.

The fifth verse of the Mandukya Upanishad says:

Verse 5: The third aspect of Atman is the field of deep sleep. Self operating in the Deep Sleep state is known as Praajna. In this third state, there is neither the desire for any gross or subtle object, nor there is any dream. In the deep sleep, the experience of undifferentiated and unified field of consciousness remains. Here, the Self is Blissful, experiences bliss, and is turned inward towards the clarity of pure knowingness and consciousness.

For most of us, our nighttime sleep feels totally natural, and we look forward to it, since it provides a welcome intermission or rest from the frantic activities of the day. It gives us an opportunity to lay aside the burdens of the world, which include our obsessive need to protect our small self—our bodies, ideas and opinions, do our work, accumulate objects, maintain our families, get our way in everything we do and what not! We know intuitively that the fading out in to oblivion of the deep sleep is very much refreshing and life-giving.

Why Deep Sleep is So Refreshing

Deep sleep is dreamless phase of sleep. It is a place of profound rest. The ego principle completely rests in deep sleep. Mandukya says that in deep sleep we go back to our source and get recharged. In the state of deep sleep, we move closest to our natural bliss of pure being-ness. Hence deep sleep is so refreshing.

Waking and the dream states are dynamic, where we find all types of forms and activities, and get involved in them. The mind remains active, as if a movie is going on. But, in deep sleep, there is silence. In deep sleep, our consciousness moves deeper within itself. Both the conscious and unconscious mind shuts down and the consciousness slips into its essence of silent peacefulness. In deep sleep we become one with our true Self. Then why do we forget this experience of merging into our true self when we wake up?

Why Does Deep Sleep Fail to Enlighten Us?

In deep sleep, we merge with our essence of pure bliss and luminosity. But when we wake up, again the form of our present bodily existence floats up in the space of our consciousness and we readily identify with that.

This happens due to our basic ignorance about our true nature, which is formless consciousness. Ignorance makes us think that we are limited by a physical boundary, and hence we have a form. The root of this ignorance exists beyond the sheath of our intellect. Hence no amount of intellectual understanding or argument can remove this basic ignorance. Only direct perception of truth is able to remove this ignorance.

In deep sleep we merge with the ground consciousness of our being. But the problem is: We move in to deep sleep with the veil of unawareness. A veil of unawareness or ignorance remains with us which do not allow us to continue experiencing our Self-essence of bliss when we wake up. Even during the deep sleep, we do not consciously enjoy our Self-nature of peacefulness. This is because, in order to move in to sleep, first we need to drift to the domain of the unconscious, where the root of the ignorance resides. And when we move from dream to deep sleep, we carry the vestige of ignorance with us. This is the reason why sleep can't not make us enlightened, though during deep sleep we unknowingly visit the same realm of love and light.

Samadhi: Aware Deep Sleep

This trace of ignorance that covers the light could be removed, if you could enter deep sleep in wakefulness, with full awareness. Then you would consciously have a glimpse of that realm of formless oneness as pure beingness, which is love in its purest expression. Is it possible to reach a sleeplike condition while remaining fully aware? It is like when your body sleeps, but consciousness remains fully aware. This is the final aim of meditation. Any and all types of meditation were designed with the aim to attain this objective; that is, to reach this state of aware deep sleep. Ancient texts of meditation have described Samadhi as aware deep sleep.

In recent times researches have been conducted on meditators, yogis and lamas to find their brain activity during deep meditative states. In two studies (Corby et al., 1978; Elson et al., 1977), brain wave activity was monitored in Tantric meditators as they sat in the lotus position and focused on the sound of a two-syllable Sanskrit mantra. Meditators were seen to produce higher amounts of alpha and theta activity along the brain's central midline. While many of the meditators became relaxed to the point where they would fall asleep, the steady alpha and theta patterns seen on the meditators' EEGs suggested that they were able to enter and maintain a mental state close to the boundary of wakefulness and sleep, yet remain awake.

With training in advanced meditation, it is possible for people to be aware of the subtle and very subtle states of consciousness to the point of being aware of the states of dreaming and even the state of deep sleep. Nowadays people are much fascinated with the subject named 'lucid dreaming', and we know that lucid dreaming is possible. During lucid dreaming people can be aware of their dreams. Just so, advanced practitioners of meditation can actually be able to maintain a form of conscious awareness of even in the formless void of deep sleep.

Deep Sleep and Death

Study of the state of deep sleep can be very much enlightening. This state is much like what happens in death. We are never afraid to jump in to the abyss of deep sleep relinquishing all our worldly cares, because we know that sleep is a normal process, it is safe and we'll lose nothing, when we wake up. But most of us will be very uncomfortable if I say that death happens to us every day when we enter deep sleep. The concept of death has remained so scary that many do not like to talk, listen or even think on the subject. It is normal, from the point of view of the individual consciousness, because self wants to exist forever. The fear of death arises in us because of the wrong notion of self. Fear of death arises because we have identified ourselves with our individual bodies, which are just transient forms appearing on us, while we are the consciousness, the energy of Om.

Deep sleep and death – both are actually a home-coming, which we all instinctively yearn for. Sleep shows us a familiar way of dissolving our bodily identity, and so, we certainly are not afraid of falling asleep. Death is unknown to the mind and hence it scares the mind. But with the practice of deep meditation, you'll see that death is like deep sleep in many respects. It is relinquishing our cares and concern to rest in our true nature as undifferentiated pure consciousness. Both in deep sleep and in death, the Self takes rest by abiding in its nature as pure consciousness. It is, as if, the wave— our body-mind and notion of individuality, becomes one with the ocean, the ocean of pure Consciousness, the God energy, which is the limitless light of existence-awareness-bliss.

Deep understanding of this process can make us absolutely fearless of death. Death is nothing but a long sleep, when we merge in to GOD, our Ground of Dwelling. Om is the loving living God that embraces us when we die. Fear of death will vanish as we shift our sense of identity from our body to our true nature as the energy of consciousness.

If we identify ourselves with the cosmic ocean of consciousness, which is the unified energy-field of Om, our fear disappears. Energy is indestructible, we know. In death, the wave becomes one with the ocean. Only our forms change, while, we remain same as the energy that 'is' and that 'knows'.

This "is-ness" and "knowing-ness" are the two basic aspects of consciousness; the "is-ness" is the existence aspect; we exist forever. The "knowing-ness" is the awareness aspect. We are aware of our existence. In death, only our forms and shapes disappear, just as our dream body disappears and merges in the energy field of our waking consciousness. But we continue to exist. We do not cease to exist when our dream body disappears along with the dream. Likewise, we continue to exist as the God energy, even after the death of the physical body. So long as the body is there, we perceive ourselves as limited beings, while actually our being is limitless. In death we become one with our essence, the formless, limitless God consciousness.

Chapter 5: Om as the Ground of Consciousness

The experience of deep sleep is like a void filled with bliss. During deep sleep, our consciousness touches the ground of the subconscious mind, but normally remains completely unaware of it.

Sl.No.	Consciousness	State	Experience
1	Conscious Mind	Waking State	Individual
2	Unconscious Mind	Dream State	Individual
3	Subconscious Mind	Deep Sleep State/ Samadhi	Cosmic
4	Super-conscious	Fourth State (Nirvana)	Transcendental

The subconscious mind is made of the energy of pure "I am", which is pure sense of existence. It is the support of all the experiences in the waking and dream state. This 'I am' is not individual. It is the same for all beings. It is the energy of pure knowing and being. It is the most intimate, innermost presence within you, that you feel as your Self, at a pristinely clear moment, when there are no thoughts in your being. It is the energy that can heal you and make you whole. This is why the experience of deep sleep is so much rejuvenating and life-giving.

Let us see what the sage of the Mandukya Upanishad says about the state where the self merges during deep sleep.

The sixth verse of Mandukya says:

Verse 6: This is the Lord of all; this is the omniscient presence. This is the inner knower. This is the source of all; this is verily that from which all things and beings originate and in to which everything dissolves.

In the third state of our consciousness we become one with God. We, all beings merge in God in deep sleep. This is consciousness in its purest state. It is Om in its purest form. Mandukya describes this field as 'the lord of all'. Om is synonymous with God. Om is the signature of the divine. Om is the signature of the universe. Om is the signature of the timeless on the temporal. Hence, when you hold Om in your bosom, in your heart, in your breath or in your voice, you are holding the signature of the infinite in your bosom, in your heart, in your breath or in your voice. You adore God knowingly or unknowingly just through utterance of the word 'Om'.

The Lord of All

In the state of deep sleep, our consciousness touches the ground of existence. This ground is pure state of knowing and being. This is the pure formless ground of the 'I Am'. It is not the individual egoistic thought of limited existence. It does not refer to a small center of awareness. On the contrary, it is the vast cosmic field where small individual 'I am' thoughts do not exist. It is the ground of whole existence. All individuality melts in this vast ground of oneness. It is the ground of unity for the whole creation.

We are separate only in the superficial layers of our being, which our unconscious and conscious minds are. The ground is same for all. It is the subconscious, which at the cosmic level is called the God, the Tao or the Buddha mind. At the level of this ground consciousness, no distinction exists. We, all of us are led back to this source at the time of deep sleep. This source replenishes and revitalizes us. This is the absolute unity consciousness that entertains no duality.

This field of consciousness is the Lord of all, because it controls all the desires of all beings and leads to its fulfillment. This essence is the only knower, as the pure energy of witnessing. It is the supreme choice maker at one level as the pure energy of volition and at another level, it is the pure creative energy that experiences itself as the 'I Am'. It creates all the material things, situations and also non-material things like thoughts, emotions and desires. It is the experience and the experiencing principle; it is the program and the programmer of our lives. It is the supreme indwelling presence in all things and beings that 'knows', creates and sustains everything. It is the supreme creator and dissolver of all.

It is the presence of God within us. We, all of us, are truly images of God. This energy of godliness is our most intimate nature. To access this Self nature of godliness is our birth-right, which we have somehow forgotten. But paradoxically, to access this cosmic 'I Am', we need to abandon our individual 'I'; we need to go beyond the individual, body-centric consciousness.

Our Infinite Supply and Power

However our small 'I's are reflection of this cosmic 'I Am', and we derive power from it. One of the greatest messages given to the human race through the scriptures is that God is our reservoir of power and that we can release our power through our spoken words. The pure 'I Am' is God's presence in human being. This is our infinite supply, from which we draw all we need.

Every day we touch this supreme presence, the non-dual ground of our existence when we sleep; but the irony is that, few of us really experience and know this state. All our desires come from this state and all our desires get fulfilled from this state. This 'I Am' is the pure consciousness that takes the shape of all things, beings and situations by flowing in to them and by identifying with those forms. Hence, those who are really aware of their oneness with this state can effortlessly fulfill and manifest all their desires.

This state of deep sleep is the state of ultimate bliss that is not dependent on any worldly object. Since the experience of deep sleep happens in complete unawareness, we forget the experience of bliss, as we wake up. If we can move in to deep-sleep in a state of awareness, we can directly experience this state of bliss— bliss that does not depend on any external object or condition.

I Am: The Source of Joy

In the state of deep sleep, we are merged in the ground of pure 'I Am', which is pure blissfulness. This level of pure 'I Am' is real and permanent, compared to the completely ephemeral state of waking and dream states. All the pleasures, happiness and joy in the waking and dream states come from this screen of pure consciousness of existence which we experience in deep sleep. This is the source of joy for all beings. Any situation, object or experience in our life gives us joy only when it pierces the veil of thoughts to point and connect us to this pure 'I Am'. Whenever our consciousness is pointed to the direction of pure 'I Am', and is connected to it, we feel joy. Whatever you love connects your consciousness with this fundamental 'I Am'-power existing within you. This is the reason why any experience of love is an unfailing source of joy.

This screen of pure 'I Am' is the same in all beings. It is the ground of cosmic oneness. Whenever you feel oneness with something, some ideal or some person, it connects your consciousness with this level, and you experience joy, with your mind erroneously thinking that the joy is coming from that object or person.

The extent of your joy depends on the intensity and duration of your connection at this level. Therefore, the extent of joy you derive from a particular object or experience depends on the intensity of your love for the object, which determines the duration your consciousness remains connected with the layer of pure 'I Am' within you. All the blissful experiences, spiritual or sensual, sacred or mundane derive their blissfulness from this layer of pure 'I Am'. In deep sleep too, connection with this screen makes the sleep experience so much desirable and refreshing, though normally we forget the experience of bliss in deep sleep, due to total unawareness during this state.

Any event of life can make you miserable to the extent you move away from this screen of pure 'I Am'.

What makes us move away from this screen? It is our thoughts and emotions that cloud the screen. Negative emotions like anger, hatred, grief or fear generally trigger a storm of thoughts that make people miserable, clouding the screen in the process.

The practice of holding on to this thought of pure being can make you free from sorrow. It can make you blissful even in the midst of adverse circumstances.

Pure Bliss of Being

Now this knowledge gives you the most wonderful treasure of your life. You know that you do not need to search anywhere for happiness, because it exists within you. Be it love, sex, food, name, fame, glory, worship or admiration, the joy in every joyful experience is derived from the same source. The source is the screen of pure 'I Am' that exists within you. This source is the energy of God. The ancient texts tell us that God is Sat (pure Existence), Chit (pure Awareness) and Ananda (pure Bliss). Bliss is the most wonderful aspect of God.

Knowledge that Can Set You Free

Now we know that the source of bliss exists not in any external object, person or situation. It exists within us— every one of us. This knowledge has the potential to make us free. When we know how to access this bliss within, it makes us free. It makes us free from the dependence on any external object, person or situation. This can bring tremendous freedom. Nothing, no external object can bind us, as we know that we are the source of our bliss. Experience of this inner bliss ushers in a new shift in our perception of this world and worldly objects. This ground of blissfulness is the experience of God within us.

Samadhi: An Experience of Uncaused Bliss

Every day we touch this most precious center of our being in the unawareness of deep sleep. However, as we have already discussed, sleep can seldom transform us, or make us wise, though it heals and rejuvenates us. It is because in deep sleep we touch the ground of our Godly being with the veil of unawareness.

What if you could access this state in complete awareness? If you could, in complete awareness, access this ground, you could have tasted an exalted type of bliss that is uncaused and independent of any external factor.

Yogis use several techniques to enter a deep sleep-like state in complete awareness and enjoy the bliss that is independent of any external object or situation. This state of aware deep-sleep is ordinarily called Samadhi. Samadhi is a blissful state of the consciousness of pure being ('I Am'). During the Samadhi, you touch and often become one with the pure blissful ground of pure being relinquishing the small 'I' experience in the cosmic ground of pure 'I Am'.

Samadhi gives you a taste of the infinite, in your ordinary life. It is the flavor of the eternally tranquil and peaceful 'now', where no thought is present to interfere. The individual I-thought and all its delusory effects dissolve into a uniform field of stillness. Practice of meditation allows you to have a glimpse of this restful silence. Long Bhramari Om chanting also helps you to rest for a while in this state and be refreshed.

Chapter 6: The Transcendental Om

Is Samadhi the ultimate experience? Or, is there something beyond that? Normally, in all spiritual literatures and scriptures Samadhi is glorified as the zenith of human experience. At this state of consciousness, there are no thoughts, and consciousness abides in a state of complete restfulness and bliss.

Beyond Samadhi

For many spiritual seekers, bliss seems to be the ultimate destination in their spiritual voyage. For those, who dare to enquire if there is anything even beyond the state of ultimate blissfulness, the seer of Truth in the Mandukya Upanishad delivers the seventh verse. This verse is for those daring seekers of Truth who dares to take any risk to know and realize the Truth, as it really is, and not as it should be.

Samadhi gives us a glimpse of the reality that is deeper than any other ordinary states. However, it is not the culmination of spiritual experience. Though many spiritual texts have eulogized Samadhi as a very exalted and desirable state of consciousness— which no doubt it is— Samadhi is not the end of the journey. It is a state which you may enter in to and come out of. Like any other experience in the world Samadhi too has a beginning and an end.

What remains beyond Samadhi? What remains when even the cosmic curtain of "I Am" vanishes in to perfect Silence? Is there complete extinction? The mind cannot provide answer to these questions, because mind is made up of thoughts. It is incapable of reporting about a state that is beyond thoughts.

Is there something that has no beginning and no end? Such a state actually exists beyond the 'I Am' thought. Still it is not actually a 'state', because it is always there underlying all the three states.

Let us see what the sage of the Mandukya Upanishad says about this.

The seventh verse of Mandukya says:

Verse 7: It is that which is neither conscious of the internal world (of mind); nor is it conscious of the external world; nor is it conscious of both. Nor it is a mass of consciousness. It is neither conscious nor unconscious. It can't be seen and it is beyond perception. It is beyond empirical or ordinary dealings. It is beyond grasp and impossible to describe by signs or attributes. It is beyond thoughts and beyond description. It can only be realized by being one with it. It is free from the world of phenomena. It is the tranquil, unchanging, non-dual and auspicious Silence. It is the fourth. It is called the Self, the essence. It is to be known and realized.

The sage of Upanishad seems to be at a loss in finding words to describe this fourth state, which is the ultimate and absolute ground of our existence. This state is indeed the most supreme super-conscious. It is the Brahman, the infinite in its absolute essence.

From ordinary states of consciousness, it may seem a bit far out though, it is the innermost core of our being. It is called the Turiya, the transcendental. This state transcends our ordinary states of existence. It is the ground on which all the three states of waking, dream and deep sleep and also the Samadhi state appear and disappear.

The Fourth state or 'Turiya' is realized when even the cosmic curtain of pure 'I Am' disappears. 'I Am' is the pure thought of being. It is the first as well as the last thought. It is the first thought. It is the mother of all forms and phenomena. It is the last thought, which, when it disappears, leaves a blessed state called no-mind. No-mind can bring us perfect liberation from all sorrows here and now. No-mind can free us from repeated chains of births and deaths.

The Transcendental Silence

The Upanishad holds the torchlight to enlighten us that all the states existing in the domain of mind are temporary. Samadhi is a transient state too. In Samadhi you touch the ground of cosmic consciousness. Even this lofty state of Samadhi is not permanent, because the experience of Samadhi happens in the domain of mind. You enter in to Samadhi, and you come out of it.

There is a state which exists beyond mind, which falls in the blessed realm of no-mind. It appears when the 'I Am' thought disappears. Like any other thoughts in existence, the pure 'I Am' thought can disappear too. When that happens, you do not cease to exist. When the screen of 'I Am' disappears, only the background of pure transcendental silence remains.

You continue to exist as a perfectly self-aware transcendental silence. You remain as a self-aware emptiness which is experienced as the pure silence of being. There is no thought, not even the thought of being. This state is difficult to describe in words. This is our true Self, the highest Self. Mandukya Upanishad says that everyone should try to realize this most auspicious state of being.

Fourth: The Ever-existing Background

The fourth State is the unchanging curtain on which the drama of life is enacted upon. It is the background that always existed behind the veil of pure 'I Am' thought. You are that background. You are that immortal and eternal Self on which everything in all the three states appears and disappears.

How to realize the fourth state of being? It can be realized in pure silence. It can appear to you if you continue to ask yourself 'Who am I?' in all your experiences of pleasure and pain. It can be realized in the clarity of awareness during deep meditation, if you are daring enough to look within your being and inquire through the veil of your 'I Am' thought. If you dare to let go of the bliss that comes along with Samadhi and dive deeper and deeper in to your being to find the source, you will find the bare face of the reality. You will find the truth in its entirety. You will find that even if the thought of being disappears in a state of perfect awareness and pure silence, you do not cease to exist. You remain as this background of pure stillness, emptiness and silence. This is your immortal Self. You are that! This is what the Buddha called the 'Nirvana', the causeless.

This is your real Self, which is absolute and immortal. You are that pure state of self-aware peace. You have always been that. You will always remain that, though the temporary states of waking, dream and deep sleep may appear and disappear on you. You are and have always been this spacious emptiness, the background of peace and stillness. All the events, all turmoil of life happen on the periphery. All turmoil happen on the domain of mind and thoughts, which is far away from this realm of peace.

Abiding in this space of pure silence makes us immune from the storms. You can be that now, this very moment, because it exists in the core of your being. You do not even need to go through any elaborate spiritual practices, rituals or austerities to be what you already are. You do not need to 'do' anything to be that. You do not need to 'become' that. This very moment you are that more than anything else you may consider yourself to be.

Nirvana: Neither Emptiness nor Fullness

To individual everyday consciousness the concept of silence is often very much misunderstood. It may seem like inert, lifeless, boring, and even scary to some. If it were like any of those experiences that numbs the senses, it won't be worth attaining. But the sage of Mandukya inspires us to try to experience it. It must be known, if you want to completely know yourself.

The enlightened ones and Buddhas of all ages permanently abide in this background state. They are never deviated from this state of eternal peace. In deep meditation, in perfect awareness, when even the 'I Am'- thought disappears, what remains is a state of absolute stillness, emptiness or pure silence that is the very ground of all that ever existed. It is an experience of the infinite and the absolute, where mind ceases to exist.

We have already discussed why this state of no mind is even greater than Samadhi. In this experience of the transcendental silence, even the thought of knowing and existing disappears. Then what remains is a blessedness experienced as a deep peace unfolding from moment to moment. Awareness remains perfect, in its supreme glory. This is when you exist as a perfect Self-aware silence. Words can hardly describe the infinite blessedness and grandeur of this state.

This is the formless infinite; this is the fourth, the transcendental aspect of Om. This is a unified field of existence that can be simultaneously experienced as blissful emptiness and an all-pervading fullness from which all forms and phenomena appear. This is what the Buddha called the state of Nirvana. This is the ultimate level of our being. The perfectly enlightened ones abide in this state.

Om: The Essence of Self-knowledge

Most people live their lives superficially. Most of us remain completely unaware of the vast reality called the Self. In the waking state of consciousness, we take our bodies as the self and during the dream state we take our dream bodies as the self. Which one is our true self? Which one is the real 'I' in us?

If we assume that the waking state is real and the dream state is illusory, why the waking 'you' cease to exist during the dream? If both the waking and dream states are real experiences, then where do you go during the deep sleep? Do you cease to exist during the deep sleep? As you wake up from the deep sleep, you find your waking body on the bed. During the deep sleep and also in the dream, only your waking body temporarily disappeared from your consciousness. Similarly, when you wake up from a dream, your dream body disappears from your consciousness and you find yourself identifying with a waking body.

So, what is it that bridges these three states of consciousness that is, the three states of your being: the waking body, the dream body and the peaceful being of nothingness in the deep sleep? What is the common cord that exists in all three states?

Ordinarily these three states of consciousness are utterly delinked for most people. They remain almost completely unaware of the fact that these three states, together with the background, make the complete reality of what we call a man or woman.

Your presence is an organic totality, which include all these temporary states, along with the permanent background on which they appear and disappear. We are pure awareness rolling on from one state to another. We ignore the totality of our being when we erroneously assume that a particular state is holding our complete identity.

The waking and dream states are like temporary movies appearing on the screen of pure 'I Am' thought, the pure consciousness that holds the gamut of all our experiences. In deep sleep, you merge with this pure thought of being— the pure existence without identification with any name or form. Ultimately, all these three states happen on the background of awareness, which exists as the eternal silence that we really are.

Chapter 7: The Sound and the States of Consciousness

After imparting the knowledge of the Self, the sage of Mandukya Upanishad again proceed to enlighten us how the syllables of Om can be linked to the three states of consciousness. Just as water (H_2O) can exist in three states like ice, water and vapor, Om can manifest itself as the three states— waking, dream and deep sleep, which are represented by the letters 'A', 'U' and 'M'.

The eighth verse of the Mandukya Upanishad elaborates on this in the following manner:

Verse 8: This Self (Atman) is Om (AUM) from the stand-point of syllables. From the stand point of letters or sound (it is viewed as) AUM. The states are defined by letters and the letters define the state. These are the three letters: A, U and M.

In the next three verses, the sage proceeds to explain how these three letters define the three states of the Self, and how this knowledge helps the knower to attain the desired things. The Self knowledge is the supreme among all knowledge, because it can lead the seeker to the attainment of supreme peace and fulfillment. It is the most desirable among all the things in the entire Universe. The scriptures say that even the gods worship a person who has gained the Self knowledge as their interior subjective realization.

However, the sage says that apart from the ultimate fulfillment of human life, the knowledge of the Self can also bring the seeker many things desirable from the worldly point of view.

The ninth verse of the Mandukya Upanishad says:

Verse 9: The field of waking state is called the Vaishvanara, and it is denoted by A, the first letter or sound (of AUM). It is denoted by A, on account of its all-pervasiveness or being the first. The one, who knows it as such, surely attains the fulfillment of all his desires, and becomes the first or foremost of all.

This is a startling revelation by the sage. We knew so far that Om is everything we experience. Then why does the sage now say that the field of waking state of consciousness is represented by the letter A of AUM or Om? Does it contradict the sage's statement in the first verse, where he said Om is everything?

Actually there is no contradiction. The sage does not contradict his earlier statement when he says that the waking state is made of by the letter 'A'. How? When we say that the ocean is made of water and again say that the ocean is made of waves, we are correct both ways; we do not contradict our statement "The ocean is made of water", when we say "The ocean is made of waves".

In the first sentence, we are referring to the ingredient that is the essence of the ocean, while in the second statement we are referring to the form aspect of the ocean. The case is the same for the following verses of the Mandukya Upanishad. When the sage says that everything is made of Om, he is referring to the essential energy aspect of the creation. When he says that the waking state is denoted by the letter 'A' of Om, he is referring to the objects included in the field of the waking state.

The letter 'A' is the waking state, which is an expression and an integral part of the Om, just as the waves are expression of and part of an ocean. In Sanskrit language, the vowels 'A' and 'U', when joined together, form the 'O'. Though actually Om is a monosyllabic sound and it is indivisible, it has been divided for the purpose of explanation.

The sage of Mandukya Upanishad explains that since this first letter 'A' is the first or foremost of all letters and pervades almost all sounds, it denotes the all-pervading state of waking consciousness, which is the first or foremost state of our worldly existence. One, who knows this state as represented by the letter 'A' of AUM, attains all his desired objects and becomes foremost among all. This is the revelation of the verse, which is a mantra seen by the sage. No intellectual analysis can stand here. The person of Self knowledge knows everything existing of the as their own Self as the energy of Om or AUM. When you know that, you know the objects of waking state as an expression of your own consciousness.

According to the Mandukya Upanishad, the objects existing in the field of waking state is an expression of letter 'A' of AUM; when you know and feel the objects of your waking state consciousness as the 'A' part of your own Self, which, in totality is denoted by AUM or OM, this knowledge enables you to attain what you desire. The vocal utterance of the letter 'A', using speech as the energy of creation, certainly creates a special sound vibration in the body and environment. This is the secret why meditation on the 'A' or 'Ah' sound is known to confer one many material benefits. Phonetically the letter 'A' can be chanted as "A-A-A-h-h-h..." This sound is known as a creative sound that helps people to manifest and attain their material desires.

BANANI RAY

Vaishvanara : The Cosmic Being

The Mandukya says that the field of your waking state is the first state of the Self, it is denoted by the letter 'A' and it is called Vaishvanara. The word Vaishvanara comes from the Sanskrit word Visva, which translates as the Cosmos. The field of our waking state or the Vaishvanara, is the first syllable of Om, denoted by 'A'.

All states of consciousness begin with the waking state. We may say that the waking state is the beginning of the other states. Likewise, 'A' is the beginning of all letters, the first syllable in the series of letters in the alphabet.

Since the verses of Mandukya originally comes from Sanskrit, it should be noted that in Sanskrit, the first letter of the alphabet is 'A', uttered as the 'A' in the English words 'All' or 'Awesome'.

In the letter 'A' all other word-formations are said to be contained, because the moment you open your mouth to speak without making a deliberate movement of the tongue, you are most likely to proceed to utter 'Ah', which is phonetically close to the sound of the English letter 'A'.

In Mandukya Upanishad, 'A' is attributed, in an apparently very peculiar way, as the first phase of the Atman (Self). However, here we must remember that Sanskrit is a very much phonetic language, where words and sounds are considered as the creative energy of the divine. So, when the sage says that the syllable 'A' is the expression of the Consciousness existing as the objects of the waking state, he actually refers to the 'Ah' sound of the letter 'A'.

When you remember that the field of your waking state is a state of your own Self, you can conceive yourself as the space that includes everything and being that you experience in your waking state. You are the field that excludes nothing you experience during your waking state. Then the whole world becomes a part of your own self. This state is the state of Vaishvanara, a state where one identifies with the Cosmos as one's own body. The Sun and the moon, the trees and the rivers, the heavens and the earth— everything exists within you, as a part of your own cosmic body. The vast wind is your breath. All your actions are cosmic movements. Your breath is the cosmic chi or vital energy. Your intelligence is the cosmic intelligence. Your existence is cosmic existence. Your happiness is Cosmic Bliss. This is a type of meditation and it leads one to a very exalted state of consciousness.

The tenth verse of Mandukya Upanishad goes on to expound the glory of the second syllable of AUM:

Verse 10: The field of dream consciousness is called 'Taijasa'. It is denoted by the second letter (of AUM); it is denoted by U, due to superiority or on account of equality. (U stands for the Sanskrit words "Utkarsha", which means Superior and "Ubhaya", which means both.) One who knows Om in this manner, he/she surely becomes superior and his/her range of knowledge equals all (means: They become inferior to none). In his/her line of descendants there is none who is not a knower of Brahman.

The field of dream consciousness is the vast reserve of the unconscious mind that stores all the past impressions as seeds of desires and Karmas. In this mantra, the sage reveals that the field of dream consciousness is denoted by the letter 'U' of Om (AUM). By knowing the objects in the field of dream consciousness as the subtle sound of the letter 'U', the knower becomes superior in his field of knowledge and all his descendants become the knower of the infinite, Brahman.

As discussed earlier with the syllable 'A', the letter 'U' is the dream state, which is an expression of the Self, just as the waves are expressions of an ocean. The subtle sound of the letter 'U' contains the unconscious impressions and the mystical knowledge of the sound of the letter 'U' is said to confer excellence and grand progeny to the knower of the Self.

The next mantra, the **Eleventh verse of Mandukya Upanishad says**:

Verse 11: The field of deep sleep is called Prājna and denoted by the third letter (of AUM). It is denoted by M, because of being limit of all, and being the state of dissolution. (M stands for the Sanskrit words 'Miter' or 'Apiter' that is indicative of measurement, limit or dissolution.) One who knows this identity of Prajna and M knows the cause and limit of the world of all things and beings and become this state where everything appears and dissolves.

We have already discussed that the state of deep sleep is the ground of consciousness which gives birth to all the other states of waking and dream. It is the ground of dissolution of all beings— a ground from which they emerge again. In deep sleep, as also in death, we are temporarily dissolved into the state of pure consciousness, only to emerge again to fulfill our residual desires.

In the blissful state of deep sleep, our consciousness almost touches its own essence of pure being. Only a small vestige of a form remains as the thought of 'I am'. One, who knows the identity of the letter 'M' and the field of deep sleep as an expression of his or her Self, becomes the knower of all.

According to the sage of Mandukya, the letter 'M' is the state of deep sleep. Phonetic importance of the sound is symbolic of the creation of a state of pure consciousness, where all forms and phenomena dissolve in to and originate from.

In deep sleep, the mind disappears, because there is not even dreaming and no content is present. In deep sleep, you have fallen back again into your true nature. In deep sleep, you are no more an ego; you are no more a hub of myriads of thoughts and emotions; you are no more an individual. You become part of the ocean, of course unknowingly, unconsciously.

If this happens knowingly and consciously, the state of oneness with your true nature becomes Samadhi, and it brings ecstasy. Mandukya says, if you know your true Self and know the significance of the syllable 'M', you'll become one with it and become a knower of the cause of the universe.

Chapter 8: Merging into the Field of Immortality

The last verse of Mandukya Upanishad describes the ultimate state of Self-realization. This verse goes on elaborately describing and extolling the fourth state of consciousness, which is the ultimate essence and glory of Om.

The twelfth verse of Mandukya Upanishad says:

Verse 12: The fourth has no parts (no sounds) and no letter can denote it. It never can be a subject of empirical dealings. All the worlds of words, letters, forms and phenomena cease here. It is the non-dual state of peaceful silence. This state of Om is the Self itself. The one who knows this state surely enters the Self by the Self (and merges their individual self in this supreme Self).

The Self described in the fourth state is none other than what we really are. It is what we are at the deepest core of our being. Mandukya Upanishad points us to our real Self.

95

But normally this is not what we believe us to be. Ordinarily we have a very different idea of 'self'.

Literally, the word 'Self' means what we really are. But at different levels of our existence, the word can mean different things to us. And if you probe deeper, you will find that all these selves are temporary and illusory in nature. They are not who you are in essence.

The False selves

At the waking state of consciousness, when you normally identify with your physical body, you call it your 'self' or 'I'. In your dream, there is another body, which is often similar with the body in the waking-state; that is your 'self' till the dream continues. Even in the waking state, we have many selves. Do you know how many selves you carry?

In different experiences and different phases of our lives, we identify with so many things. Whenever we identify with something or someone with thoughts such as 'This is me' or 'This is mine', a new self is born. It exists till that 'something' or 'someone' exists and till we identify with it.

Such a self is ever-changing. For example, when you identify yourself with your body, what happens? This moment your 'self' is thin and fair, and in a couple of months you may find your 'self' a shade or two darker and gaining some weight, if you happen to take a long holiday to a tropical island, where you eat, drink and relax on the beach without any workout.

Similarly we often identify ourselves with our vocation as a lawyer, a doctor, a professor, or a manager. What happens if we do so? A lawyer-self, a doctor-self, a professor-self or a manager self is born. It will die the moment you quit your profession. Or its remnant may continue with the prefix 'ex', as 'Ex-professor' or 'ex-manager', which is actually another self.

Similarly when you identify with a child, a mother or father self is born. It was not there when the child wasn't there. Suppose you adopted the child. The child was growing in an adoption center. Your father or mother self was born the moment you identified with it as 'This is mine'. This happens not only for physical objects but for mental ideas as well.

When you identify with a thought, an idea, an ideology or an opinion, you identify with your subtle mental body. Then a self is born within you that asserts itself as the owner, creator or follower of that idea, opinion or ideology. Deep identification with a mental idea of a certain religion or a certain idea of God gives rise to religious fundamentalism. Deep rooted identification with a certain sect gives birth to narrow sectarianism. When somebody, identifies with a sect to such an extent then that sect becomes his or her self.

Then anybody criticizing that sect becomes the object of wrath of that person who identifies with it.

All these selves are not your real selves. These small, narrow selves are products of ignorance. They are just 'concepts', concepts of who you are. They are false ideas about who or what you are, and they are temporary.

Just because they are mere concepts or ideas, these selves are ever-changing and transient in nature. This moment they are here and the next moment they are not. The child-self in you that was afraid of ghosts is no longer present in you as you have grown up. Do you see why those changing selves were never your true reality?

The Funny Debate: Self or Non-self?

Our temporary selves go on changing every moment. The small selves die the moment the perishable objects of this world perish, while the real you remain unchanged among this constant change.

Our small selves die many deaths every moment, because constant change is the nature of the universe. Nothing— no form or phenomenon is permanent here. This is the reason why the forms and phenomena in the waking and dream states and also the small self born of identification with them was declared by the Buddha as non-self (or Anatta, meaning, not the real Self). Buddha described the ultimate changeless substratum as the Nirvana, which the Mandukya points as the fourth state.

The Truth remains the same, whether it is contained in the Vessel of the Upanishad, or Buddhism or any other philosophy, for that matter. Only those that did not experience the Truth as their own subjective experience goes on debating and fighting about whether there is a self or no-self is the reality of the Universe.

Many Buddhists fall in the same trap as the Hindus, when they mindlessly accept emptiness and no-self as a general doctrine or dogma, just as their Hindu counterparts often wrongly assume that the individual self found in the waking state exists forever.

The simple truth is this: That, which is limited by a form or mental concept, or is associated with a form or mental concept, perishes in time, because change is the nature of this existence.

Then what is the presence within you that remains changeless? The formless self-aware silence within you is the substratum. This is what is your real Self, the Self distinguished by the 'S' in uppercase. Ordinarily we, humans go through our life utterly oblivious and unaware of this presence that is our real Self. This real Self, this background presence is called the fourth or *Turiya* in the Mandukya Upanishad.

Nirvana in Daily Life

I am sure, many of my readers are wondering about the usefulness and relevance of this knowledge in our daily life. We need to eat, we need to do our jobs, we need to interact with our friends and colleagues and we do need to take care of ourselves and our family. Don't we? Doesn't the Fourth state sound too lofty for our ordinary daily life and mundane daily activities?

Sure, it does; but I can assure you that being aware of your innermost Self in the midst of your waking experiences will lead to an amazing life-experience, and it surely is possible. Witnessing is the gateway to the Fourth state.

The Witnessing Presence

The energy of witnessing is an amazing presence that exists within us. Witnessing happens when you watch things as an aware presence without identifying with the objects of your observation. And it is lost the moment you are identified to anything— a thought, an idea or a person. Identification often brings sorrow in the long run. Practicing the witnessing to your changing selves that appear in various states of your experience and various phases of your life brings blessedness.

The witnessing presence is the substratum and also substance of the three states— waking, dream and deep sleep. This presence within you takes you from waking to dream state, from dream to deep sleep and again wakes you up from the deep sleep to bring you back to the waking state. If there were not this background presence, we would be completely identified with the states, and we could never come back from the deep sleep.

The waking or dream and deep sleep states are mere mirage, passing phenomena on the pure consciousness, which is the innermost witnessing presence. Being aware of the existence of the formless witness of the three states within you will liberate you from deep rooted identifications.

If you continue with this practice, then a day will come when the blissful experience of existing as a 'no-I' (no-self) formless presence will start penetrating your waking and dream states. Then it will be easy to have frequent small glimpses of the forth state, the Turiya, the Nirvana.

When this state will start penetrating and overlapping your waking and dream states, you will see good health and peace of mind happening to you effortlessly.

Blessings of Realizing the Fourth State

Mandukya Upanishad gives you the master key for health, happiness, peace, serenity and fearlessness. A simple understanding of the fourth state, which is your real Self, can initiate a silent revolution in you.

By applying this wisdom and understanding in every situation of your life, you will experience a powerful cognitive shift in the way you view the world, respond to it, receive information and process it. You will find increasing clarity in your thoughts and decisions, and your relationships will improve as a result. When your waking and dream states are constantly illumined by the fourth state, it is called living perfect enlightenment.

The Bliss of Perfect Fearlessness

Everywhere in our earthly existence is wrought with fear. In youth, there is fear of old age and disease. In old age there is fear of death. In prosperity there is fear of losing it. In poverty there is fear of starving. There are fears of failure, fear of loss of relationship, fear of losing our loved ones, fear of rejection, fear of ignominy, and the list goes on. When you turn on the switch of your TV, everyday you are faced with news of some natural calamity, corruption and terrorism, which inculcate fresh fear in your mind. A vast majority of the humankind is living their lives in fear-consciousness, a very low vibratory state. And the worst thing about it is that fear is contagious like any other emotion. It makes the scenario bleak.

Fear is the worst enemy of humankind, because it lives by generating more of its kind. The world needs more and more people that live in courage, love and gratitude. The vibratory state of just a handful of such people can compensate the ongoing vicious circle of fear. Courage is the beginning of a spiritual consciousness.

The wise men of the east say that fear of death lies at the root of all fears. The study of the wisdom of Mandukya and its practical application in our lives can come to our rescue. When we are identified with that eternal essence of our being, we conquer the fear of death. What is beyond death? The witness is beyond death. The self-aware pure silence is beyond death. So, when we identify with Om or the pure silence following the sound, we reach the deathless. We become perfectly fearless. The bliss and beauty of this state of perfect fearlessness is beyond words. This state can be perfected by continuous practice.

Essence of Immortality

Om or AUM in its totality is our immortal Self, our immortal being. Om constitutes of the letters A,U,M and the Silence that follows uttering the word. The parts (viz. different transitory states of consciousness) fall in the domain of death. Only the whole is beyond death. What is the whole?

The whole has two aspects. First is the essence of the sound uttered as a monosyllable. Truly Om is uttered as a monosyllable with a nasal sound following O. This monosyllable Om sound is the witnessing silence. This is one aspect of the whole— the energy aspect.

The other aspect of the whole is the pure silence that follows the utterance of O_O_O_O_O_ M_M_M_M.....The witnessing silence gradually grows in to pure silence, the fourth, the Turiya or Nirvana.

However, the paradox is that, the parts and the whole exist together. The parts have never been separated from the whole, just as the waves have never been separated from the ocean. It is only our conditioned mind that ignores the whole, which is the totality of our existence. It is our conditioned mind that grasps only a part of our experiences as our complete self. Our conditioned mind erroneously thinks the body appearing at a particular state as our complete self. Through the mindful study of Mandukya Upanishad, by attuning to the vibration of Om and by practicing witnessing, one can break away of the conditioning of the mind.

When this conditioning is erased out, you realize the vast and limitless essence of your being. You realize immortality, while being in this very body. You remain rooted in your essence of oneness; you abide in limitless love, joy and blessedness. That is the eternal state of Om. That is the true nectar of immortality, drinking which you become immortal.

Chapter 9: God in Our Daily Life

To see a world in a grain of sand
And a heaven in a wild flower,
Hold infinity on the palm of your hand,
And eternity in an hour."— William Blake

The Essence of Mandukya: Seeing God Everywhere

Every now and then, we come across a person or a situation where we can see or feel the presence of God. Often we recognize it a few moments after the encounter, and it is only on reflection that we realize that something extraordinary happened to us; we feel that God has touched our lives in some way.

If you meet someone who regards mankind with compassion and who is accepting without judgment, you will recognize that God is near you. All-encompassing love is a reflection of God. A spontaneous act of kindness kindles a flame in our heart that never goes unnoticed as divine. Everywhere in this creation there is the signature of God. Yet we miss it. We miss it because we too easily segregate life into the categories of sacred and mundane.

Mundane, everyday events can be viewed in a deeper dimension if we can acknowledge that we are part of an extraordinary intelligence that pervades this cosmos. Our existence is sustained by every breath God gives us. Our existence is sustained by the God-essence within us. There is great freedom if we get to the place of seeing that views all of life belonging together. No matter where we are, there is God; — Not a God who judges and bestows reward or decrees punishment; not a God who loves us more when we are doing something 'spiritual' and who loves us less when we are engaged in mundane activities, but a God who will never judge us, because God has created us in his/her own image and perfectly knows why we are the way we are; a God that loves us unconditionally and can't do otherwise because it is God's own Self that has manifested as us. Such a God cannot divide our goodness from our badness, because unconditional and non-judgmental love is what God is.

The study of Mandukya Upanishad widens the arena of our mind. We know such a God not only exists but is as real as we are, because God exists as the core of our being, as our essence. We are living at a time when human consciousness has been evolved to a stage where a grand leap towards the infinite is not only believed to be possible in the arena of consciousness, it has been real to many people belonging to different cultures from all walks of life. In this context the study of Mandukya has become most relevant than ever.

How do we discover God in our daily life? When we live our life mindful of the godly essence within us and other human beings, plants and animals in our environment, we discover God within us, in our daily life. You may start by becoming mindful of the godliness or God-presence in any human being— it may be your lover, your parents or your co-worker. It may be someone who lends you a helping hand during a moment of crisis. It may be your wife or husband who brings for you a wonderful meal or a cup of tea prepared with love and care. It may be your children who greet you with warm love and smile when you are back home from work after a stressful day. It may be anybody and everybody. God is playing in this world in the mask of a human, a puppy, the morning Sun or even a daffodil that lights up the field.

We think we eat, drink and do things. Doesn't God eat in us? Doesn't God live in us? Mandukya teaches us to start looking at God's creation as the manifestation of God. Om is the living God that manifests as this universe.

When we are gentle and kind, and start seeing the spirit of God working everywhere, within everybody, our talks, our breaths and our lives become divine. We should always become aware of the fact that we represent God, and that will make us bright and beautiful and divine.

Everything that exists in this world exists for a reason— God has manifested as that to light up somebody's world. We need to honor the uniqueness of every being, as we should honor ours. We are unique as everything in this creation is. We have a reason to exist. The moment we are born, God has chosen to manifest as us. We should feel honored for that.

When you start honoring the light of God within you, and within other human beings, suddenly one day you feel the horizon of your view opening up. You find a puppy and feel that God is playing through its fluffy mask. You find a nightingale singing on a tree, and you see God.

If you live in this way, you will find yourself becoming more sensitive to the God's gracious and loving spirit in your everyday life. The more you feel and know God's gracious and loving presence in your everyday life, the more you will become a person of love and grace to others and your life will become a symphony of celebration.

Aligning with the God Consciousness

Om is the living God and we align with the God consciousness when we align with Om. How do we align with Om? We align with Om by saying "Om" and lending a helping hand to our fellow travelers on this journey on the earth. We align with Om by meditating on Om as the eternal song going on within us. We align with Om when we find it in the innocent giggle of a baby or unadulterated laughter of a child. We align with Om when we pay attention to our inner silence.

The Honey of Immortality

The honey bee gathers nectar from the flower making the continuous humming sound by its wings and it transforms the nectar in to honey. When you say Om again and again, especially the long ones, your consciousness gets focused and concentrated. The dross is removed in the process, and the consciousness gets more and more refined like the honey. You become full of peace and light. Chanting Om and attuning with the sound can transform your ordinary consciousness into the honey of immortality.

The Legend of the Humming Bird

Humming birds have been considered sacred by many people, especially by some ancient civilizations. When they fly, hover and move quickly with their wings flashing illusive patches of shimmering colors, the humming birds seem like flying fleck from a rainbow that glows and hums. In Vedic civilization the humming birds were thought divine. It was because they were thought to symbolize a heavenly spirit that is not earth-bound. Did the humming of their wings remind the sages of the sound of Om?

It is said that humming birds can induce a state of metabolic dormancy, which makes it look like it is immersed in a trance or deep meditation. Many Native Americans believe that this symbolizes humming bird's ability to live on the borderline of life and death. Ancient Andean and Indian Sun-worshippers believed them to be a transformed form of the Sun God. They have legends that say that hummingbirds float free of time, eternally carrying hopes, love, joy and celebration.

Notwithstanding their lack of scientific truth, these legends are beautiful, and humming birds are a joy to see, no doubt about it. If you listen to the musical hum of its wings, as it rises and falls in sweetest cadences, you can't help but think that the bird is chanting Om-m-m-m-m-m…. while gathering honey from the flowers.

Can the birds open our eyes and inspire our imagination? The humming birds can inspire us to utter the sweet Om, feeding on the honey of immortality and living as a beauty, a grace and joy to the world.

God appears as many manifestations in this creation teaching us many sublime truths of this grand existence. There are many instances in the Upanishads, where the birds, beasts and even the elements taught wisdom to the sages. We just need an open heart, a clutter-free mind and clear eyes to see. Worshipping the living God in Om can make our life a piece of joy and a blessing on earth. It can lead us to such a point where we can feel that beauty is everywhere, every personal connection has meaning and that laughter is life's sweetest creation.

May all the beings attain to and ever abide in that eternal realm of sublime peace that passes all understanding. May all beings realize true peace in their hearts. May peace pervade the whole existence. Om Peace, Peace, Peace.

The End

Annexure

The Mantras of the Mandukya Upanishad

Verse 1:

Hari Om. Om ityetad aksaram, idam sarvam; tasyopavyakhyānam, bhutam bhavad bhavisyad iti, sarvam omkāra eva. yac cānyat trikālātitam tad apyomkāra eva.

Translation: *Hari Om. Om, this immortal sound, is all that exists. It is the past, it is the present and it is the future. All that exist are really expressions of Om. And whatever transcends the three spheres of time, that too is indeed Om.*

Verse 2:

Sarvam hyetad Brahman. Ayam ātmā Brahman. So ayam ātmā Chatushpāt.

Translation: *Om, this immortal sound, is all that exists. It is the past, it is the present and it is the future, all that exist are really expressions of Om. And* *whatever transcends the three spheres of time that too is indeed Om. Everything in this whole creation is Brahman, the Infinite. And this self too is Brahman, the infinite.*

Verse 3:

> Jāgarita-sthāno bahish-prājñah saptānga
> ekonavimsatimukhah sthūla-bhug vaiśvānarah
> prathamah pādah.

Translation: *The field of waking state is conscious about the externals. It has seven limbs and nineteen receptors. It receives, consumes and enjoys gross subjects (sensory inputs). This first state is known as Vaishvanara.*

Verse 4:

> Svapna-sthāno antah-prājñah saptānga
> ekonavimsatimukhah praviviktabhuk taijaso
> dvitīyah pādah.

Translation: *In the Dream state, the Self is conscious about the   inner world. This* second state is known as the Taijasa. It operates through seven limbs and nineteen gates to experience and enjoy the subtle objects of the mental realm.

Verse 5:

Yatra supto na kancana kāmam kāmayate na kancana svapnam pasyati tat sushuptam. Sushupta-sthāna ekibhūtah prajñāna-ghana evā-nandamayo hyānanda bhuk chetomukhah prājnah trityah pādah.

Translation: The third aspect of Atman is the field of deep sleep. Self operating in the Deep Sleep state is known as Praajna. In this third state, there is neither the desire for any gross or subtle object, nor there is any dream. In the deep sleep, the experience of undifferentiated and unified field of consciousness remains. Here, the Self is Blissful, experiences bliss, and is turned inward towards the clarity of pure knowingness and consciousness.

Verse 6:

Eṣa sarveśvaraḥ eṣa sarvajñaḥ, eṣo'ntaryāmi eṣa
yoniḥ sarvasya prabhavāpyayau hi bhūtānām.

Translation: *This is the Lord of all; this is the omniscient presence. This is the inner knower. This is the source of all; this is verily that from which all things and beings originate and in to which everything dissolves.*

Verse 7:

Nāntaḥ-prajñam, na bahiṣ prajñam, nobhayataḥ-
prajñam, na prajnāña-ghanam, na prajñam,
nāprajñam; adṛṣtam, avyavahāryam, agrāhyam,
alakṣaṇam, acintyam, avyapadeśyam, ekātma-
pratyaya-sāram, prapañcopaśamam, śāntam,
śivam, advaitam, caturtham manyante, sa ātmā, sa
vijñeyaḥ.

Translation: *It is that which is neither conscious of the internal world (of mind); nor is it conscious of the external world; nor is it conscious of both. Nor it is a mass of consciousness; It is neither conscious* nor unconscious. It is unseen and beyond perception. It is beyond empirical or ordinary dealings. It is beyond grasp and impossible to describe by signs or attributes. It is beyond thoughts and beyond description. It can only be realized by being one with it. (It is the essence of the realization of oneness). It is free from the world of phenomena. It is the tranquil, unchanging, nondual and auspicious Silence. It is the fourth. It is called the Self, the essence. It is to be known and realized.

Verse 8:

so'yam ātmādhyakṣaram auṁkaro'dhimātram pādā mātrā mātrāś ca pādā akāra ukāra makāra iti.

Translation: This Self (Atman) is Om (AUM) from the stand-point of syllables. From the stand point of letters or sound (it is viewed as) AUM. The states are defined by letters and the letters define the state. These are the three letters: A, U and M.

Verse 9:

Jāgarita-sthāno   vaiśvānaro-'kāraḥ   prathamā mātrā-'pterādi mat tvād vā-'pnoti ha vai sarvān kāmān ādiś ca bhavati ya evaṁveda.

Translation: *The field of waking state is called the Vaishvanaro, and it is denoted by A, the first letter or sound (of AUM). It is denoted by A, on account of all-pervasiveness or being the first. The one, who knows it as such, surely attains the fulfillment of all his desires, and becomes the first or foremost of all.*

Verse 10:

Svapna-sthānas taijasa ukāro dvitīyā mātrot-karṣād ubhayatvād-votkarṣati ha vai jñāna-santatiṁ samānaś ca bhavati nāsyā-brahmavit kule bhavati ya evam veda.

Translation: *The field of dream consciousness is called 'Taijasa'. It is denoted by U, the second letter (of AUM);*

it is denoted by U, due to superiority or on account of equality. (U stands for the Sanskrit words "Utkarsha", which means Superior or finely cultivated and "Ubhaya", which means both.) One who knows Om in this manner, he/she surely becomes superior and his/her range of knowledge equals all (means: become inferior to none). In his/her line of descendants there is none who is not a knower of Brahman.

Verse 11:

Suṣupta-sthānaḥ prājño makāras tṛtīyā mātrā miter apīter vā minoti ha vā idaṁ sarvam apītiś ca bhavati ya evaṁ veda.

Translation: *The field of deep sleep is called Prājna and denoted by the third letter (of AUM). It is denoted by M, because of being limit of all, and being the state of dissolution. (M stands for the Sanskrit words 'Miter' or 'Apiter' that mean measure, limit or a state of*

119

dissolution.) One who knows this identity of Prajna and M knows the cause and limit of the world of all things and beings and become this state where everything appears and dissolves.

Verse 12:

*Amātraś caturtho-'vyavahāryaḥ prapañco-paśamaḥ
sivo'dvaita evam Oṁkāra ātmaiva, saṁviśaty
ātmanā-'tmānaṁ ya evaṁ veda ya evaṁ veda.
Iti Māndukyopanisad samāptā.*

Translation: *The fourth has no parts (no sounds) and no letter can denote it. It never can be a subject of empirical dealings. All the worlds of words, letters, forms and phenomena cease here. It is the non-dual state of Silence. This state of Om is the Self itself. The one who knows this state surely enters the Self by the Self (and* *merges the individual self in this supreme Self).*

Here ends the Māndukya Upanishad.

Om śantih; śantih; śantih!
(Om Peace! Peace! Peace!)

ABOUT THE AUTHOR

Banani Ray is a mystic, spiritual guide and author of several books on meditation, mysticism and infinite human potential. She studied and mastered the Bhagvad Gita, when she was in school, and the book became her constant companion. She adored and took Bhagvad Gita as her guide. While she was teaching in a women's college, she experienced an awakening, and underwent a massive inner transformation, which led her to undertake deep spiritual practices in the quest for realization of the ultimate truth.

Ultimately, her quest motivated her to undertake austere spiritual practices and self-enquiry in solitude. For several years, she lived in Himalaya with her husband Amit, living a life dedicated to meditation and spiritual practices. Over the years, a series of mystic experiences opened up for her the door for profound realization of the underlying connectedness and oneness of all beings. She began to live her realization, sharing her wisdom and teachings with people coming to her from far and near.

Also from Inner Light Publishers

Awakening Inner Guru: The Path to Realizing the God Within by Banani Ray and Amit Ray

 This book is a clear and straightforward guide to awaken the light within. For those who are truly interested to attain spiritual freedom and fulfillment in every sphere of life, this book is a practical and personal manual.

Om Chanting and Meditation by Amit Ray

 Om is our blissful Self. Om is the mysterious cosmic energy that is the substratum of all the things and all the beings. It is the eternal song of the Divine. This book makes the Om meditation easy to follow, simple to do, and very effective.

ISBN: 9788191026931

13957925R00074

Printed in Great Britain
by Amazon.co.uk, Ltd.,
Marston Gate.